Foreword

The Black Country has a proud history of manufactu~ of the Industrial Revolution, right through to the post-Second ~~ in coal extraction following events such as the 1926 General Strike began the decline in the fortunes of the region. This was followed after 1945 with nationalisation, principally of two major steelworks: Round Oak and Spring Vale (later known as British Steel, Bilston). This nationalisation was reversed by a subsequent government, but Bilston closed in 1980 and Round Oak in 1982. In my opinion both closures were politically motivated, and began the rapid decline in British steelmaking.

Some time after the closures, Dennis Turner MP stood on the terrace of the Houses of Parliament watching the central steel hub of the London Eye being shipped up the Thames. It had been made in Hungary. Further irony is that in 1968 the last deep mining operation in the Black Country closed; the UK now imports most of its coal from overseas, by 2008 43.9% of coal used in the UK came from overseas. The decline of coal as a fuel for power stations has since diminished and more coal-fired power stations are being decommissioned.

This book paints a picture of one family's work in the iron industry in a much earlier period than that I describe above, but the industry was still subject to boom and bust, as you will see when you read it. What it does is to provide a chronology of the business, but, more unusually for a book of its nature, covers the working conditions and lives of many of the men and women who worked for the Rose family. At the back of the book a handy appendix lists all the names of those people mentioned in the book, and why their names have been recorded. This social history aspect will be welcomed by local historians, genealogists and students of social history in equal measure.

The family's fortune and progress was not always smooth; as was common across the region and the country. Boom and bust plagued Black Country industries, war often brought boom, but in peace time the bust hit hard. Strikes were also common; in the mines these could have catastrophic effects, flooding meant many pits had to close after being assessed as being uneconomical. There were bankruptcies in 1857 and 1881, but also expansion, partly due to the growth of the railways, in the period of 'Railway Mania'.

The Rose family first came to prominence as ironmasters in the Moxley area in the early 19th century. Daniel Rose developed as an entrepreneur; but the book focuses on his youngest brother, David, who by 1870 employed over 450 men. Other family members also feature such as their brother, William, and cousin, Thomas Rose. Accidents, Health and Safety, welfare, industrial relations and Charitable Giving all have their place in the book, sometimes in contrast to other books on industrial subjects; there is something here for everyone.

British Library Cataloguing in Publication Data
A catalogue record for this book is available from the British Library

ISBN 978-1-911309-05-5

Typesetting & Origination by Mike Pearson **editor@blackcountrysociety.co.uk**

Printed in Great Britain by iPrint, Leicester.

The Black Country Society

The term 'The Black Country' was coined in the mid-19th Century to describe that area of the South Staffordshire coalfield where the 'thick coal' lay.

Over 150 square miles some 100 small industrial communities developed and by the late 1890s a couple of dozen of them were of sufficient size, perhaps when linked with some of their neighbours, to have their own local councils. Since that time there have been several local government reorganisations and after that of 1974 all of the townships of the Black Country were absorbed into the four Black Country Metropolitan Boroughs of Dudley, Sandwell, Walsall and Wolverhampton. In December 2000 Wolverhampton was granted city status.

The Black Country Society was founded in 1967 by enthusiasts, led by Dr John Fletcher, who felt that the Black Country did not receive its fair share of recognition for its great contribution to the industrial development of Britain and the world.

The Society grew out of the Dudley Canal Trust Preservation Society which had successfully campaigned to save Dudley Canal Tunnel which had been threatened with closure by the British Waterways Board and British Rail. The preserved tunnel linking the Birmingham Canal System and the canals of the Stour Valley, with links to the River Severn, is now a major attraction at the Black Country Living Museum.

The stated aim of the Society is to 'foster interest in the past, present and future of the Black Country'. Its voice calling for the establishment of a local industrial museum at a meeting on 6 October 1968 was one of the first on the subject.

Contents

Introduction

Financial meltdown, banking collapses, economic depression, workers' unrest, social deprivation, imbalance of wealth, environmental concerns and newspaper reports of salacious family scandals are not subjects confined to the early 21st century. This study of a 19th century family of industrialists encompasses all these.

The origins of this book lie in a venture into family history and a story that my late mother (nee Martha Rose) told of our family connection with Darlaston industrialists. The work focuses on the Rose family who first came to prominence as ironmasters in the Moxley area in the early 19th century. It examines the rise of the Black Country iron industry and how Daniel Rose developed as an entrepreneur. While it also makes reference to his brother William and cousin, Thomas Rose, it focuses on his youngest brother, David, who by 1870 employed over 450 men.

The work attempts to set the Roses' concerns in the light of the developments in both the coal and iron industry in the period. It looks at how the family was caught up in the frequent financial crises of the 19th century. It demonstrates how the ironmasters created networks through which they controlled the market, secured supplies and kept abreast of technological advances.

It also examines the impact of the Rose concerns on their employees, particularly the dangers and challenges faced by both colliers and ironworkers in their working environments. It focusses on the disasters afflicting the works of David, Daniel and Thomas Rose, some of which finally led to action on boiler safety.

It looks at the relations between the Roses and their workforce, how they treated their employees, often embodying the patronising approach of the age while at the same time squeezing every last drop of blood from them. It follows the workers' struggles for social justice and how these struggles affected the Roses. In addition it examines the impact of their collieries and iron factories on the living conditions of their employees and highlights, through a series of case studies, the desperate acts that many of them were driven to.

It seeks to demonstrate that the financial irregularities and speculation of the early 21st century are nothing new. It reveals lessons for us in contemporary Britain where the distribution of wealth is increasingly unequal, where the rhetoric of 'helping hardworking families' belies the trend to benefit those who have wealth in abundance. And most of all, it demonstrates how hard won were the living and working conditions that we now take for granted.

The story is not without family scandal as it traces how David Rose's son was caught up in a classic upstairs-downstairs relationship. It touches upon the circles that the Roses moved in and the lifestyle they developed and examines the collapse of all the Rose concerns and the legacy for the area.

I would like to thank the staff at Walsall Local History Centre, Sandwell Archives, Dudley Archives, Wolverhampton Archives, Birmingham Library and the Staffordshire Record Office for their help in sourcing both documents and images. I am also indebted to Mary Harding, another descendent of the Roses, for providing additional information and support. In addition, I am grateful for the support of the Black Country Society in this venture and in particular to Mike Pearson, for his very practical assistance.

1. The rise of the Black Country iron industry and the origin of the Rose family's iron connections

The rise of the Rose family goes hand in hand with the early history of the iron industry in the Black Country. The Black Country is an area of South Staffordshire which was one of the major centres of heavy industry in Britain from the late eighteenth century. The term 'Black Country' came into use in the 19th century as a description of a particular smoky and sooty area. The first recorded usage of the term 'Black Country' comes in a speech, given in November 1841 to a Reformers' meeting, by Mr Simpson, the Town Clerk of Lichfield. The first published use of the term can be traced in a children's book by the Reverend William Gresley, who described it as a 'dismal region of mines and forges.'[1]

The area lies over a huge coalfield, known as the 'Thirty Foot Seam'. Most of the coal seams rest on a bed of fireclay, while seams of iron-stone occur throughout the coalfield. Elihu Burritt, the American consul in Birmingham in the 1860s observed that: *'Nature did for the ironmasters of the Black Country all she could; indeed, everything except literally building the furnaces themselves. She brought together all that was needed to set and keep them in blast. The iron ore, coal and lime – the very lining of the furnaces – were all deposited close at hand for the operation ... In some, if not all, parts of this remarkable region, the coal and lime are packed together in alternate layers in almost the very proportion for the furnace requisite to give the proper flux to the melted iron. Thus Nature has not only put the requisite raw materials side by side, but she has actually mixed them in right proportions for use ...'* [2]

By the 17th century the mining of iron had become a considerable industry. The various Black Country communities eventually developed their own specialised metal trades. Willenhall produced locks while Cradley Heath became a chain-making area and Wednesbury became known as 'tube town'.

John Wilkinson

One of the key figures in the early history of the iron industry was John Wilkinson who in 1756 had settled in nearby Bradley, near Bilston, Staffordshire and established a blast furnace for the smelting of pig-iron.

Wilkinson gave a powerful impetus to the use of coke-smelting. Coke, made from coal, had already begun to supersede charcoal as a fuel when Wilkinson introduced it at Bradley in 1757. This united the two main resources of the area - coal and iron. His works built on two of the three key elements in the take-off of the Black Country iron industry. First, Wilkinson improved Henry Cort's puddling furnace and rolling mills. Second he made Boulton and Watt steam engines and installed at least twelve in his Bradley works. Their power was used for blowing furnaces and forges, winding coal, lifting hammers and working rolling and slitting mills. The third factor was the building of canals. Nearly all of the forges and mills of the area, including the works of Daniel, David, William and Thomas Rose, were built on the banks of a canal. Wilkinson's ironworks ushered in the age of the factory, although many trades, like nailing, continued on a domestic basis until the later 19th century.

1. The *Staffordshire Advertiser*, 27th November, 1841. Rev. William Gresley, *'Colton Green: A Tale of the Black Country'*, 1846
2. Elihu Burritt, *'Walks in the Black Country'*, 1868, p.2

An iron industry fuelled by war

The late 1790s and early 1800s were a boom time for the iron industry. Not only had key breakthroughs been made in its technology, but also the demand for iron products was growing, fuelled by the French Wars. Between 1793, when war broke out with France, and 1796 the price of iron had remained steady. The increased output of British works and the imports of iron from Sweden and Russia enabled supply to keep up with demand. However, between 1795 and 1801 the price of Russian and Swedish iron increased from £14 to £25 per ton and duties on foreign iron increased by nearly a pound per ton, between 1796 and 1798. In addition, at the end of 1800 trade between Russia and Britain was suspended with the possibility of war. These were the key factors in stimulating English iron production.[3]

It is against this national and international picture that we first come across the Rose family's involvement in the industry at the Deepfield Ironworks, just a mile from Bradley. Scrivenor[4] notes that in 1796 there were fourteen blast furnaces in the Black Country including one at Deepfields. The first documentation connecting the Rose family to the iron industry comes in the registers of the Coseley Old Meeting House Presbyterian Church, close to Bilston, where on December 24th 1802, the birth of Henry Rose is recorded. It reveals that his father, William, was the Head Slitter at the 'Deepfield Iron Works'.[5]

Henry Rose's birth, recorded at the Old Meeting House, Coseley, showing the occupation of his father, William. (Courtesy Dudley Archives & Local History Service)

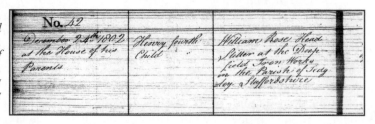

The Deepfield Ironworks were part of the Earl of Dudley's estate which centred on Sedgley, Dudley and Brierley Hill. The Earl had extensive coal mines and had developed canals and a rail network. The blast furnaces, forges and rolling mills on the estate were all leased to tenants. The Deepfields Furnaces were run by George Stokes in partnership with Samuel Pemberton, Benjamin and Thomas Stokes. George Stokes was a nail ironmonger and ironmaster of Oldwinsford and Kinver Mill who also owned mines at Rowley Regis.[6] William Rose and Elizabeth Tingle were married there in 1797[7] and this may be how William came to work at Deepfields. With all the new furnaces, and their associated undertakings came a demand for labour which could not be satisfied locally and workers were often pulled in from surrounding districts.

The nail industry had a long history in the Black Country and, although we know little about the occupations of earlier members of the Rose family, we know that Elizabeth was the daughter of John Tingle who was born in Ecclesfield in Yorkshire. Both Ecclesfield and Rowley Regis were nail manufacturing areas and we might speculate that the two families met via their connections with the nail trade.

3. TS Ashton, *'Iron and Steel in the Industrial Revolution'*, pp.143-146
4. H Scrivenor, *'History of the Iron Trade'*, 1854, p.96
5. Dudley Archives, CO84501, 1792-1815
6. R Shill, *'South Staffordshire Ironmasters'*, 2008
7. Rowley Regis Parish Registers, Marriages 1754-1812, volume 6

A slitting mill, such as the one William Rose worked in, processed iron bars, rolling them into a strip and passing them through slitting rolls which produced nail rods. As head slitter, William would have had a supervisory role in the process. Gale[8] states that, *'The whole mill was driven by water power. Iron bars were first drawn down to a suitable size under the tilt hammer and were next rolled into strip in the plain rolls. The strips were then passed through the slitting rolls, which slit them into nail rods. Various sizes of rod could be produced by varying the thickness of the strip and by adjusting the number and width of the slitting collars. The slitting mill came to be an important part of many Black Country ironworks.'*

A slitting mill pictured in Popular Science Monthly, January 1891

Henry was one of several children born to William and Elizabeth Rose. There are records for a Daniel, William, James, Elizabeth and David.[9] William would have been more than capable of supporting his family as the English iron trade continued to boom in this period. A Shropshire ironmaster reported to the Committee on the Coal Trade in December 1800 that:

'There are new furnaces for the smelting of iron constantly erecting; and it is now difficult to get pitmen to work the Coals.'[10]

Although peace with France was signed in October 1801 it did not have a huge effect on the English iron industry. In 1802 another 22 new furnaces were in blast and 25 more being built. War broke out again in 1803 with Russia throwing in her lot with France. Thus shielded from foreign competition, the English ironmasters were able to sell the output of their furnaces and forges for very remunerative prices. By 1806 there were 42 furnaces in South Staffordshire and a dozen of these were on the Dudley Estate.[11]

Even Napoleon's blockade at first had very little impact as alternative export routes were found. However there was an American embargo on British goods from late 1807 to March 1809 which led to a general trade depression. During the early days of the embargo nails and sheet iron were smuggled in via Canada. Nails were an important article of exportation to America where the use of wooden buildings occasioned a widespread demand for them. William and his fellow slitters would have benefited hugely from this.

By 1811 however a deep depression had really hit the iron trade, but William did not live to witness it. The registers of the Old Meeting House at Coseley record his burial, aged 35, in May 1811. While other entries record cause of death, there is no reference to how William died, so we can only speculate that it may have been due to an industrial accident. However, the knowledge that he had gained in the industry was to lay the foundations for the growth of one of the biggest family firms in the Black Country. His sons Daniel, David and William were all to become leading ironmasters.

8. WKV Gale, *'The Black Country Iron Industry'* 1966, p.14-15
9. St Leonard's Baptismal Registers, Bilston
10. From the Committee on the Coal Trade, December 1800, quoted in TS Ashton, op.cit. p.142
11. TJ Raybould, *'The Economic Emergence of the Black Country'* 1973, p.137

2. Daniel and David Rose's early ventures as entrepreneurs at the Moxley Forge

Daniel Rose was the eldest son of William and Elizabeth Rose and was born in 1799. He would have been 12 when his father died. Thus the responsibility of being the 'man' of the family would have been thrust upon him at a very young age. Daniel took his youngest brother David, born in 1810, under his wing and both were later known as being proud to have been self-made men. William may have already introduced Daniel to his work at the Deepfields Ironworks, which would have provided an invaluable education for him in his development as an ironmaster. The next time we come across Daniel is in December 1823 when he marries Mary Penrose in Sedgley. Their only child, Martha, was christened at Darkhouse Baptist Chapel, Coseley on 24th November 1824. Having no son to pass on his assets to was perhaps another factor in Daniel's mentoring of David.

The period following the end of the French Wars in 1815 was one of depression. For a third of a century the economy of Britain had been stimulated by the wars with France and industrial output had greatly increased. Following the advent of peace there were fewer government contracts and prices fell. Few men were prepared to chance their arm and risk new industrial ventures. However, ten years after his marriage, Daniel was running the Moxley Forge near Wednesbury, a few miles from Deepfields. His younger brother David, aged 23, was already involved in the business and by 1837 was managing the works. Circumstances had changed and were more favourable to new initiatives.

How did Daniel start his business?
During the 1820s there was a 50% increase in the number of blast furnaces erected in South Staffordshire - mainly in Tipton & Bilston. By 1830 the Black Country equalled South Wales and surpassed Shropshire as a centre of finished iron production. It was the beginning of the area's dominance in the iron trade. By 1850 one third of the national output of wrought iron was made in the Black Country and pig iron production expanded by 300% between the years 1830 and 1858.

However, the period from 1825 to 1832 was still one of uncertainty and it is no coincidence that the first reference to Daniel Rose's business is in 1833 when he took advantage of the end of the downturn in trade to begin work at the Moxley Forge. Staffordshire iron prices reflect the growth of the industry in this early period. In 1832 pig iron sold at £3 per ton. By 1833 this had risen to £5.10s and bar iron to £8 per ton. Technical advances began to lead to increased productivity, reduced costs and improved the quality of iron.

Daniel Rose had to start on a small scale and was therefore typical of the many small iron and coal masters of South Staffordshire in this period. Gilbert Gilpin, a contemporary ironmaster and former manager employed by John Wilkinson, wrote, *'In Staffs. landed property is very much divided and naturally all the proprietors are desirous of turning their coal and iron mines to immediate account. Hence, there is a colliery in almost every field. As there is no sale for such an immense quantity of coal and limestone, several of these little proprietors unite together to build furnaces; clerks from the neighbouring manufacturers are taken in as partners to direct the concerns; the tradesmen of the town in the vicinity who can raise a 100 or 200 pounds form part of the firm, and it is in this way that the ironworks have been multiplied in that county. The proprietors embark all their property and all that they can borrow in these establishments.'*[12]

12. Dowlais MSS, G Gilpin - JJ Guest, 3 October 1819

In 1815 Thomas Butler, a Yorkshire ironmaster, noted that in the Black Country, where coal was readily accessible, there was a tendency for a rash of small pits and furnaces to develop, operated by small coal and ironmasters[13]. Birch[14] says that there were four sources available for initial investments: The landowner, who might begin iron production himself, retrenchment and retention of profits, merchant capital and loan capital – usually from bankers. The development of both Daniel and David Rose's businesses demonstrates all of these bar the first.

The Moxley Forge

Moxley Forge, at Bulls Bridge, was well located, being on the banks of the Walsall branch of the Birmingham Canal, enabling raw materials and finished products to be easily transported. The documents relating to the Moxley Ironworks give an idea of how and when Daniel got started: leasing land, working in partnership with others and obtaining finance from the Bilston and District Banking Company.

The first evidence we have of Daniel in business comes from a 'schedule of deeds', dated 1849[15]. This records that on 16th September 1833 an agreement was made between Isaac Johnson of Moxley, a cooper, Edward Maybury, a clothier of Bilston, James Hartlan, ironmaster of Wednesbury and Daniel Rose. This concerned an assignment of leases of the premises of Moxley Forge and 'stock in trade.' Maybury and Johnson appear to have been sleeping partners and when, later in the month, the partnership with Hartlan was dissolved, Daniel was running the business.[16]

The pace of expansion and development can be gauged from an agreement that Daniel made in December 1833 with Edward Dolman Scott of Great Barr Hall and Baronet Edward Thomas Foley of Stoke Edith Park in Herefordshire, for the lease of the land on which the forge stood, for a period of 42 years. The agreement stated that Daniel was to use no less than 20,000 good bricks when constructing his buildings.[17]

In 1834 Daniel Rose made a further agreement with Maybury, borrowing £150 from him at a rate of 5% by mortgaging his share of the lease.[18] In April 1840 the mortgage agreement was discharged and thenceforth Maybury appears to no longer to have a stake in the works.[19] The growth of the business can also be judged by the fact that the Moxley Forge, under Daniel's name, made its first appearance in a Trades Directory in 1839.[20] That this was very much a family concern is borne out by the roles played by Daniel's two brothers, David and Henry.

David abroad

While Daniel was laying the foundations of the business we begin to get a glimpse of David's prowess and his education as an industrialist from his children's birth certificates. When his son, Henry Rose, was born in July and baptised in August 1837, he was living in Darlaston and listed as a 'manager of ironworks'[21]. However, two years later at the age of

13. Thomas Butler, *'Journal of the Tour in Staffordshire'*, 1815
14. Birch, op.cit. pp. 198-199
15. Staffordshire Record Office (S.R.O.), Papers of Addison, Jesson and Cooper, Solicitors of Walsall, D1317/1/11/1/15/1
16. London Gazette, September 1833
17. Birmingham City Archives, Scott of Great Barr MS 3883/655
18. D1317/1/11/1/15/1 op. cit.
19. S.R.O. D1317/1/11/1/15/1
20. Robson's Directory of Birmingham and Sheffield 1839
21. S.R.O. D1317/1/11/5/4

28 he was living and working abroad. David's next son, William Napoleon Rose, was born in Couillet, Belgium in August 1839 and David is described as a 'marteleur' (literally a 'hammerer').[22]

What was he doing there? By this time Couillet was a major centre for the manufacture of iron in Belgium. Indeed one of the witnesses to William Napoleon's birth was Benoit Joseph Wauthy an ironmaster of Couillet. Belgium was the second country after England to go through an industrial revolution. During the early 19th century European industrialists from several countries visited England to monitor progress and to see how they might be able to replicate such rapid expansion. Sometimes they persuaded managers working in a particular industry to go back with them and act as advisors.

One of the foremost English families in the development of Belgian industry was the Cockerills. William Cockerill developed the mechanisation of the Belgian textile industry while his son John established iron works at Seraing in 1817. By 1830 these works were employing 2500 men. British inventions and technical skill were of considerable importance in the development of Belgian manufacturers. Two other Englishmen were also heavily involved in the growth of the country's iron industry. Thomas Bonehill built rolling mills in the Charleroi district while Harold Smith erected rolling mills for the nearby Couillet Company in 1835. A contemporary article described the ironworks there as, *'truly magnificent, covering more than eleven acres of ground. All the structures are well-built and exhibit a good deal of taste, as well as skill, in their designs... The furnaces at Couillet are forty-five feet high and fifteen feet across the boshes. The blast is usually hot and it requires an engine of sixty horses power to work one furnace....The rolling mills and forges are very extensive and embrace the latest of the most approved English and German improvements.'*[23]

Perhaps this is why David Rose is to be found there in 1839. The period up to1837 was one of great prosperity in the Belgian iron industry with pig iron production around 150,000 tons per annum. His presence in Belgium may have also been connected with the country's railway development. The most important early Belgian railways were national lines built by the government with Belgian firms supplying most of the equipment - but British technical knowledge and engineering skill played a part. Later, when private companies began to build railways the co-operation of British capitalists and contractors was secured. In 1845 eight private companies were founded in London to facilitate the expansion of the Belgian railways and £6 million pounds was subscribed in Britain for the construction of these lines. A railway project in the Acoz valley was begun in February 1846: *'for the purpose of putting the metallurgical establishments of Couillet and Chatelneau into direct communication with the mines.'*[24]

It is also possible that David was attempting to secure business for the Rose brothers. However, 1839 marked the beginning of a period of depression in the Belgian iron industry with production down to 88,000 tons and 36 of its 58 blast furnaces were idle for the next three years.[25] Despite the downturn, David's sojourn was not a short one. His next son, George Alexander Rose was also born in Belgium - in September 1841.[26]

22. S.R.O. D1317/1/11/5/4
23. Journal of the Franklin Institute, 1841
24. London Daily News, 5th February 1846
25. Mining Journal, 1842
26. S.R.O. D1317/1/11/5/4

A French connection

Indeed David Rose and his family appear to have been on the move on the continent for several years. Another son, James Alfred Rose, was born at Arras in France in April in 1844.[27] David's presence there again may have been linked to the development of the French railways. In 1833 the French Minister of Public Works had set up a commission to study future French railway routes and engineers were sent to Britain and the USA to examine recent developments in that area.

English promoters and contractors were active in the development of French railways for twenty years and indeed, the Moxley Forge was producing railway axles at this time.[28] In 1843, which saw the opening of the Paris Rouen line, a group of English railway developers visited northern France and it is possible that David was attached to this party. The Black Country connection with the French iron industry is well documented. Aaron Manby, owner of the Horseley Ironworks at Tipton, established a foundry at Charenton, near Paris, and took many families from the region to work there. There are also several newspaper articles of the period which document Black Country artisans moving to France to work in industries there.

By 1845 David was back in England and was taken into full partnership of the Moxley Ironworks by Daniel in that year. On the 4th June of that year there was an agreement with the Bilston District Banking Company in both their names.[29] All the trade directories of this period now refer to both Daniel and David when listing the Moxley Ironworks. As well as railway axles they were described as manufacturers of 'general use forge steam packet shafts, cranks, shafting and iron of every description.'

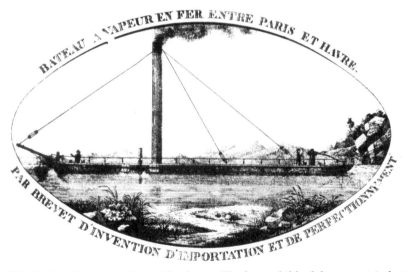

The Aaron Manby the first steamship built of iron. The brainchild of the eccentric but far-seeing naval officer Captain (later Admiral) Charles Napier, who conceived the idea of a fleet of steamships for service on the River Seine. Named after the master of the Horseley Ironworks, Tipton, where she was pre-fabricated to a design jointly formulated by Captain Napier, Aaron Manby and his son Charles. *(Courtesy Black Country Society Archive)*

27. S.R.O. D1317/1/11/5/4
28. Kelly's Post Office Directory, 1845, p.531
29. S.R.O. D1317/1/11/1/15/1

3. Railway mania and the expansion of Daniel and David's business

The period 1844 to 1846 was one of great increase in British iron manufacture, largely due to the growth of the railway network. There had been heavy investment in railway development after 1830 following the success of the Liverpool to Manchester line. The railway boom, in the sense of financial speculation, had broken in 1836 but although many proposed railway schemes were abandoned, many were carried through. Construction continued, reaching a peak for completion in 1840.

Until this time most iron was sold in semi-finished form to other ironworks for further refining, or to iron merchants, many of whom purchased it for export. With the railway boom, finished iron was now supplied direct to customers. Several other local firms, besides the Rose brothers, manufactured items for the railway industry such as Round Oak near Brierley Hill and Patent Shaft & Axletree of Wednesbury. The Bank of England, after the discouragement of the years down to 1842, was prepared to provide loans at a low interest rate. Investors, so long starved of profitable outlets, noted the success of lines built in the 1830s and rushed to sponsor new undertakings.

Purchase of the Eagle Ironworks

The Rose brothers bought the Eagle Ironworks around the mid-1840s to take advantage of this expansion. The works had been owned by Maddock and Gill, whose partnership was dissolved in January 1842 with the firm having succumbed to the depression of the late 1830s and early 1840s.[30] The contents of the works had been sold off in October 1842[31] with the sale of the buildings and equipment coming later. In 1845 the Rose brothers managed to secure a loan from the Bilston and District Banking Company, probably to assist their purchase and development of the Eagle Iron Works. Daniel and David also raised funds by offering for sale two pieces of land, called Upper and Lower Tranter's Rough, together with two cottages in June 1844.[32]

The management of the works was put in the hands of Henry Rose, Daniel and David's brother, who had also followed in his father's footsteps in the iron industry. When Henry's children, William, Martha and Jane, were christened at Christchurch in Coseley in 1836, 1842 and 1845, Henry was described as a slitter[33] living in Hall Green. However, when his last child, Esther, was christened at Christchurch in August 1848, Henry was described as 'Manager of an Ironworks' and living in Darlaston. His grounding in the industry and his family connection obviously made him a preferred choice for the running of these works.

That the market was rising is evidenced by the reports of the Midlands quarterly meetings of ironmasters in the *Wolverhampton Chronicle*. The meeting on April 17th 1844 resulted in prices being increased by about 15%. In January 1845 they were raised by a further 10 shillings a ton and in April a further increase of £2 per ton was agreed. In September 'circulars were issued by several firms announcing that they could not receive further orders unless at an advance of £1 per ton.'[34]

---

30. *London Gazette*, 7th January 1842
31. *The Birmingham Gazette*, 10th October 1842
32. *The Birmingham Gazette*, 3rd June 1844
33. Christchurch Parish Registers, Coseley, CO37861
34. *The Wolverhampton Chronicle*, 10th September 1845

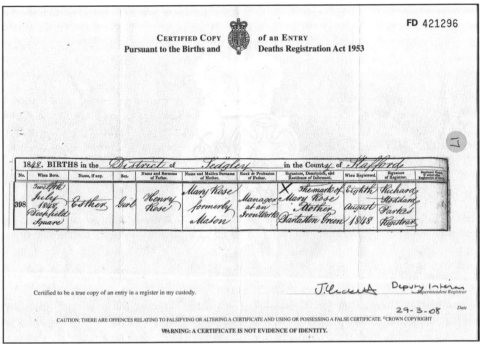

Esther Rose's birth certificate

By January 1846 the picture was even healthier: *'masters have received important orders: and the iron market was consequently buoyant, the last quarter's prices being fully confirmed with a tendency to rise. The price of bar iron was £10 per ton.'* [35] In June 1842 it had been half that price. The boom continued throughout the year and in September it was reported that: *'The present state of the iron trade in the South Staffordshire district is as satisfactory as it has been for many years past. The very extensive and increasing demand for home consumption for carrying out the various railway projects, with the requirement of the export trade, are calling into requisition all the improved facilities of production, and must keep them fully employed for many years. The order books both at the larger and smaller works are well filled with orders.'* [36]

Yet while the area was heavily involved in producing iron for the railway market there was a marked absence of local railway lines. By the mid-1840s it was imperative that the Black Country should no longer be denied the benefits of a main railway link. The Grand Junction Railway by-passed the area to the east while the London & Birmingham Railway terminated at Birmingham. Even at this stage of development some raw materials were being imported into the area and the existing canal links were proving costly in time, particularly in the case of the movement of finished iron goods from the Black Country to the ports.

Two rival schemes were projected in 1844: one was the London, Worcester and South Staffordshire Railway, running north to south across the Black Country between Birmingham and Wolverhampton. The other was a broad-gauged railway, known as the

35. *The Staffordshire Mercury*, 14th January 1846
36. *The Birmingham Gazette*, 9th September 1846
For an in depth look at this period see, JG Worpell, *'The Iron and Coal Trades of the South Staffordshire Area, Covering the Period 1843-1853,'* West Midlands Studies 1X, 1976

Oxford, Worcester and Wolverhampton Railway running south-west to north-east to Wolverhampton. In September 1845 the Manchester Courier carried an advert for the issue of shares in the latter company, described as 'the Rugby, Warwick and Worcester Railway'. Both Daniel & David Rose are listed as supporters along with many other local ironmasters.[37]

The brothers were not content just to back the one horse. Another advert appeared later in the month promoting the merits of the South Staffordshire Junction Railway as: *'the line best calculated to serve the important Mining, Manufacturing, Trading and Agricultural Interests of the Districts'*[38]. Included in the list of supporters were Daniel and David Rose. In the end a commission decided in favour of the Oxford, Worcester and Wolverhampton line. Even so, by 1850, the other line was constructed as far as Dudley, running eastwards through Wednesbury and Walsall.

The Roses were set to profit on three fronts from these developments. First, the prospect of having a wider access to raw materials and the opportunity to dispatch finished goods more quickly; second, the potential of more orders for iron products associated with new rail networks, and third, financial returns from owning shares in railway companies.

The peak of railway building activity was reached in 1847 when nearly 6500 miles of railway were under construction. By the 1850s the main skeleton of the British rail network had been laid down. The speed at which it was constructed was quite phenomenal and it could not have happened without an iron industry with a tremendous capacity for expansion. The Rose brothers were part of this phenomenon.

The railway boom then continued abroad and brought new markets into play. Yet as Birch says, the large-scale flotation of railway companies and the prospect of unlimited

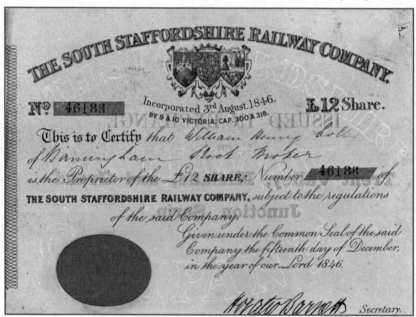

A share certificate of the South Staffordshire Railway Company. (From the author's collection)

37. *The Manchester Courier and Lancashire General Advertiser*, 6th September 1845
38. *The Derby Mercury*, 17th September 1845

orders for railway iron, led to a general attitude of over optimism and expansion of production.[39] By late 1847 the boom had begun to turn into a depression. In December it was noted that:

> *'The suspension of railway construction is working out its disastrous effects in this neighbourhood. The money panic has partially subsided, but its effects are evidenced and continued in the course which most railway companies have found themselves compelled to adopt. Orders for rails have been countermanded to a very large extent and as a consequence establishments principally occupied in trail making are pushing into the bar and other departments of the business'.*[40]

1848 proved to be a hard year for the iron trade and in January there was a widespread strike which went on for nearly three months, which must have brought both the Moxley and Eagle Ironworks to a halt. Some still struck an optimistic note: *'Profits, when obtained, are manifestly re-invested in the business in an extraordinary degree. No fact can be plainer, for new firms in the iron trade (of late years at least) are unknown; old firms, or old establishments rather, have disappeared. Yet we have an almost unimaginable extension of the trade. The impetus of the railway schemes of 1845 and 1846 is still felt, and there has recently been some slight revival in railway demand. There is, too, a constant absorption of iron for railway purposes, independent of rails; and this amount, unless railways by thrown out of use, cannot recede, but must, as railways increase, increase with them.'*[41]

By the beginning of 1849 things had indeed begun to improve slightly, but not until 1852 did the iron trade really begin to pick up again, though by this time Daniel and David had gone their separate ways.

Black Country engine c 1850

39. A Birch op.cit.
40. *The Wolverhampton Chronicle*, 22nd December 1847
41. *The Mining Journal*, 17th June 1848

4. New Partnerships

As a result of their success up to now, and perhaps also due to their individual ambitions, Daniel and David dissolved their partnership at the Moxley and Eagle Ironworks in May 1849 and went their separate ways. Daniel kept control of the Moxley Ironworks while David took on the Eagle Ironworks. This section will look at Daniel's partnership with David Skidmore and David's partnership with Richard Westley Fletcher. It will also be appropriate here to examine their cousin, Thomas Rose's, partnership.

By late 1849 Daniel was positioning himself to develop his business. In early December, Daniel was discharged from an earlier mortgage with the Bilston Bank and two days later signed another agreement with its trustees whereby he mortgaged the Moxley Forge premises for £2,000.[42] In 1850 Daniel leased more land by Bull's Lane Bridge from Scott & Foley at a yearly rent of £41[43] and by1851 he was employing 50 men[44]. By1852 the Moxley Ironworks had 8 puddling furnaces.[45]

His standing in the community was also recognised in this period. In 1855 Daniel was one of the Grand Jury members at the Staffordshire Quarter Sessions.[46] He was also named as a trustee of the Ebeneezer Baptist Church in Coseley, the foundation stone of which was laid by Samuel Groucutt, another local ironmaster, in 1857.[47] The church had hot water pipe heating as well as cast iron windows.

Daniel Rose and David Skidmore

The early 1850s saw a revival of the iron industry and by late 1852 there was a positive boom. In December 1852, the *Wolverhampton Chronicle* reported, *'The staple of this neighbourhood is now in an excited state. At the last iron-masters' meeting pig iron was declared to be from £3 15s to £4 per ton ... Since then there has been such an influx of orders that it has led the ironmasters to demand higher prices, and many of the leading houses will not take any more orders unless at quarter day's prices which they think will be at £9 per ton, if not £10, for bars. The anticipation has led the pig iron makers to ask for £4 10s per ton, and this price in some cases has been given'.*[48]

The price increase in iron naturally led to a relative price increase in coal. This was nothing new but those who controlled the collieries would obviously be in a position of influence in the iron trade. A week later the same paper reported: *'Owing to the great scarcity of coal in this neighbourhood which still prevails, the ironworks have not yet been got into full operation. Very extravagant prices are being realised for this article of consumption.'*

What both Daniel and David Rose came to realise was that in order for their iron works to develop and prosper, they needed control of a prime ingredient – coal. In 1854 Daniel

42. S.R.O.D1317/1/11/1/15/1
43. S.R.O. D1317/1/11/1/13
44. 1851 Census for Darlaston
45 List of Mills and Forges of South Staffordshire, 1852; Records of the School of Mines and of Science, vol 1 part 2, 1853
46. *Staffordshire Sentinel and General Advertiser*, 1st December 1855
47. *Black Country Bugle*, 10th June 2004
48. *The Wolverhampton Chronicle*, 1st December 1852

Rose went into partnership with Daniel Skidmore, another Darlaston ironmaster, and a William Griffin to purchase the Moorcroft Colliery which was owned by the Scott & Foley Estate. It was a 52 acre site and included a number of houses and cottages. They bought the mines for £33,000 and had to pay royalties on all ironstone and coal. A down payment of £2,000 was required and the remainder was to be paid in lots of £750 every 6 months.[49]

While the early 1850s were a boom period in the iron industry the period 1855 to 1860 was not, as will be evident when we examine David Rose's concern. Daniel Rose's business, however, was healthy until the mid-1860s with few causes for concern, but even so he was affected by the struggles of other ironmasters. In June 1860 a bankrupt nut and bolt manufacturer of Dudley, Mr W James, defrauded Daniel out of £144 by apparently tearing out pages from his cash book to give a false impression of his financial status. A court case ensued.

> 'Mr Page ... stated that he was manager of the iron works at Moxley, belonging to Mr Rose. In October last, the bankrupt came to the works and enquired the price of certain descriptions of iron. He was told so much per ton, and for cash, subject to 2 and a half percent discount. He agreed to the terms, and said he had had one transaction with the house before for cash.
>
> He then showed him his bank-book, in which there was a small balance in his favour. He (Mr Page) remarked that it was a small balance, upon which the bankrupt said his money was locked up in his works, but as he would receive cash for the iron when it was delivered in London, he could pay cash. Upon that representation, he sent the iron and called for the cash in due course, but the bankrupt said he could not pay; he called again, and received the same answer. The bankrupt asked him to take a bill for a month. Mr Rose consented, and before it came due the bankrupt was sold up.'[50]

The apparent success and stability of the Rose and Skidmore partnership was evident in an article which appeared in 1864: 'On Saturday last Messrs. Rose and Skidmore, ironmasters of Moxley and Wednesbury, gave their workmen a most liberal entertainment. The workmen, after proceeding through the village, headed by the Excelsior Band, proceeded to a spacious tent and partook of good old English fare. Mr David Skidmore occupied the chair, supported on either side by Mr Daniel Rose, and the Rev. P Wilson, and other friends. After the usual toasts, the men retired into the fields and amused themselves with several games, of which football was the favourite. Mr Skidmore also presented the children of the village with buns.'[51]

The description paints a picture of a partnership in rude health. The same could not be said of David Rose's joint venture with Richard Westley Fletcher in the 1850s.

David Rose's partnership and Richard Westley Fletcher

We have seen how David moved from being a manager in his brother's ironworks in 1837 to being a partner of the Moxley Ironworks in 1845. By 1850, after dissolving his partnership with Daniel, he began to branch out beyond the Eagle Ironworks on Darlaston Green. In July 1850 David Rose bought the Albert Ironworks in Moxley from Edward & Josiah Creswell.[52] These were located just a few hundred yards from the Moxley Forge.

49. Birmingham City Archives: Scott of Great Barr MS 3883/756
50. *Birmingham Gazette*, 30th June 1860 and Birmingham Daily Post, 29th June 1860
51. *Staffordshire Advertiser*, 30th July 1864

Edward Cresswell and Sons were coal masters at Moxley Colliery and Edward was also a manufacturer of bar iron at the Tipton Iron Works.[53] To make the purchase, David took out a loan of £10,000 from the Wolverhampton and Staffordshire Banking Company.[54]

In 1851 David was listed as the owner of the Albert Ironworks at Moxley, making sheets and boiler plates.[55] 1851 was, in many ways the highpoint of industrial Britain. It was the year of the Great Exhibition at Crystal Palace where English manufacturers proudly displayed their products. The Black Country supplied most of the iron and glass for the construction of the building, and, while there is no record of the Roses supplying their wares, they would have been amongst the six million visitors to the site.

In the early 1850s David purchased several parcels of land and mines. Railway expansion continued and the companies involved remained the greatest users of iron. With an increase in iron output, up went the demand of coal. In May 1854 David bought a piece of land called Corweths Croft together with the mines and minerals underneath. Further purchases included the Flaunch and a close of land called Coal Pit Flat.[56] Part of the Great Moxley Field was bought from Scott & Foley in December 1854 for £1,365 9s 4d.[57] Even more land was purchased in April 1857 at Cockheath, in Moxley, from William Lees and Thomas Bill for £1,938 2s 6d. David Rose had 11 shares out 24 of the land and its coal and ironstone.[58] However, by far the biggest acquisition came in partnership with Richard Westley Fletcher.

Richard Westley Fletcher was part of the Walsall firm of Samuel Fletcher and Sons, merchants, ironmongers, dealers and chapmen. The partnership had begun in 1850 and their first venture was the leasing, in 1851, of the Victoria Ironworks at Leabrook, in Wednesbury.

Leabrook Ironworks, from a postcard in the author's collection

52. S.R.O. D1317/1/11/1/18
53. Kelly's Post Office Directory, 1845
54. *The Birmingham Daily Post*, 4th December 1857
55. Slater's Directory, 1851
56. S.R.O. D1317/1/11/1/10/1-16
57. S.R.O. D317/11/4/3
58. S.R.O. D317/1/11/11/4

Poster advertising the sale of land purchased by David Rose in 1854.
(Courtesy Staffordshire Record Office)

A description of the works appeared in August 1854: *'The VICTORIA WORKS comprise a FORGE with large helve, harness, anvil and block, camring and shafting, about eighteen forge, mill, ball, annealing, and heating furnaces, a train of bar and train of plate rolls, with housing spindles, coupling boxes, crabs and bed-plates; three pairs of boiler-plate and bar shears, roll-bed lathe, complete; main shafting, with powerful driving and fly-wheels, the whole being driven by a ponderous condensing STEAM ENGINE, of eight-horse power, with for egg-end boilers; also several bundling and fagoting benches, lot of pen plates, an immense quantity of furnace fore and floor plates, standing plates, & c; several sets of pig and other scales and weights, and a WEIGHING MACHINE, with inside lever, up to eight tons.*

The Buildings comprise engine-house, forge and mill walls, with immense slate and iron roofings over the same; warehouses, offices, machine-house, stable, and gig-house, clay-house, smith's shop, three cottages, pattern shop, boundary walls, with large entrance gates from main road into a spacious yard for pigs, calcined cinder, and loose stock; also about five boats' length of wharfage'.[59]

The works contained 14 puddling furnaces.[60]

The market still appeared buoyant. In 1852 the price of bar iron was £4 17s 6d a ton but during 1853 it rose to £8 10s per ton. This was the signal for Fletcher & Rose's biggest purchase and the one which was to nearly bring David Rose's business to a premature end. The two men bought 135 acres of the Bradley Colliery for £99,000. £3,047 was to be paid on an annual basis.[61] To help make the purchase, Fletcher & Rose took out a mortgage from the Wolverhampton and Staffordshire Banking Company for £10,000.[62] Where they sourced the rest of the money is unclear. The two men were obviously ambitious but were soon to discover that they had overreached themselves.

Bradley Colliery, showing the pillar and stall mining method.

59. *The Birmingham Gazette*, 7th August 1854
60. List of Mills and Forges of South Staffordshire, op.cit.
61. *The Morning Post*, 7th December 1857
62. S.R.O. D1317/1/11/1/9/8 and D317/1/11/1/18

In trouble

During 1855 the partnership with Fletcher ran into trouble. The writing appears to have been on the wall in mid-1854 when an advert appeared for the sale of the Victoria Ironworks at Leabrook, which were eventually bought by the Patent Shaft Company.[63] Why Rose and Fletcher did not see out the remaining two years of their lease is not known, but it may be that they were already feeling overstretched.

1855 was a hard year for the iron industry. In January 1855 there were 114 furnaces in blast but by April the number had dropped to about 90. The knock-on effect was that there was less demand for coal, which resulted in a reduction of colliers' wages and a subsequent strike. The state of the industry was recorded in April 1855 when a meeting of local coal and iron masters received a deputation from the colliers of the district. The report includes details of the fall in iron prices. At the end of 1854 the price of pig iron was £5 10s a ton and by April 1855 it was £2 15s.[64]

Many ironmasters ran up serious debts and the Fletcher Rose partnership was one of the biggest offenders owing some £73,000.[65] Several meetings of their creditors were held and eventually an agreement was reached whereby the partnership was to pay a sum of 7s 6d in the pound. The money was to be paid in five instalments at four, eight, twelve, eighteen and thirty months. George Smith, the manager of the Shropshire Bank, Edward Wright and Thomas Hook Pemberton, three of the largest creditors, were appointed as inspectors to oversee the transactions.[66]

The partnership of Fletcher & Rose was not the only one to suffer at the time but similar to many firms in difficulty, with the support of local banks, they were able to carry on in business. However all of David Rose's possessions had to be handed over as security to the administrators, including mines and minerals, pieces of land at Cock Heath, the Albert Ironworks and six houses, including his own with all his household goods.[67] While this appeared to be a serious setback for David Rose, things were to become much worse.

The 1857 banking crisis

Fletcher & Rose carried on for another two years. The Albert Ironworks seemed to be doing well and in October 1857 was listed with 21 puddling furnaces.[68] 1857 had been a good year for the industry with 155 out of 180 blast furnaces being in operation, but in October there was a sudden downturn when the price of iron fell dramatically and several firms were caught out. The *Staffordshire Advertiser* published a list of 69 blast furnaces which ordinarily gave employment to 28,000 persons in these districts. On the 31st December 1857 they were all out of work.

On November 24th Fletcher & Rose filed for bankruptcy. In the five or six years preceding 1857 many new firms like Rose & Fletcher had been formed in response to expanding trade, carrying on an enormous traffic on slender capital. Banks had stretched their lending powers and the crisis of 1857 was probably the most severe ever experienced. The Bank of England found in November 1857 that its reserve fund stood at £1,552,686

63. *The Birmingham Gazette*, 7th August 1854
64. *The Staffordshire Sentinel*, 28th April 1855
65. *The Staffordshire Sentinel*, 28th April 1855
66. *The Wolverhampton Chronicle*, 15th August 1855
67. S.R.O. D1317/1/11/1/9/8
68. *The Staffordshire Advertiser,* 3rd October 1857

and its securities held against advances amounting to £30,000,000. The Government was forced to suspend the Bank Act and permit the issue of bank notes in excess of bullion.

The Wolverhampton and Staffordshire Bank, which had loaned £20,000 to Fletcher & Rose in two instalments, was a local example of the problem. The bank owed £350,000 and needed £400,000 to continue trading. The domino effect exhibited by the crisis was summed up by Mr G Robinson, a solicitor acting for the Wolverhampton Bank: *'when I mention that all, or nearly all, these estates are but so many links of one chain – that says if B, C, and D had not failed I should be on my own legs – that of B says if A, C, and D paid I could pay – that C says if A, B, and D pay I am right – that D says if A, B, and C meet their bills there is nothing the matter – that each of them lay the blame on the others.'*

Robinson outlined the policy which its depositors favoured which the bank had to follow to regain its footing: *'We feel bound to realise estates in utter insolvency if there is nothing to fall back upon, or no security for the present assets or promised profits.'*[69]

The firm of Fletcher Rose was one of those central to the Wolverhampton Bank's predicament. On December 3rd a meeting of the partnership's creditors was held when a very detailed financial statement was produced by the firm's accountants, Ryland and Chapman. Fletcher & Rose owed £40,466 and their assets were £21,322. These figures appear to be in relation to the ironworks and, while very detailed, may have been intended to confuse. In addition, there was the matter of Bradley Colliery. Of the £99,000 that Fletcher & Rose had agreed to pay in instalments, £81,000 was still owed. The partnership's solicitor, Mr Duignan made an offer to pay 12s 6d in the pound over a two year period. The offer was accepted, the estate was assigned to inspectors and arrangements were made for the partners to appear before the Bankruptcy Court. Among the inspectors appointed were Neil Solly and David Groucott – two local ironmasters.[70]

The Wolverhampton & Staffordshire Bank threw doubt on the figures that Fletcher & Rose had provided. The firm admitted that they had taken £8,500 from their present creditors to pay the old ones and the bank reckoned that Fletcher & Rose were £20,000 worse off than when they had first got into difficulties in 1855. The bank argued that Fletcher & Rose had possession of 165 acres of the Bradley Colliery and that a large proportion of the creditors' money had been invested in its development and that profits from the colliery in the coming years would enable the partnership to pay 20 shillings in the pound.[71]

The strength of feeling at the time was reflected by one newspaper which used the phrase *'amongst the worst cases of reckless trading and of trading without capital'* to describe Fletcher & Rose's business.[72] The strength of feeling may well have been exacerbated by the revelation that David Rose's salary was over £1000 per annum and that of Fletcher, more than £1400.[73]

A Private Sitting for Fletcher & Rose was held on 28th January 1858 at the Birmingham Court of Bankruptcy to determine proof of debts and to obtain the assent of three-fifths of the creditors to a proposal of future payments.[74] How well this administration of the Fletcher

69. *The Birmingham Gazette*, 28th December 1857
70. *The Birmingham Daily Post*, 4th December 1857
71. *The Birmingham Daily Post*, 22nd December 1857
72. *The Sheffield Independent*, 5th December 1857
73. *Birmingham Daily Post*, 4th December 1857
74. Birmingham City Archives, Bateman- Scott papers, 762

& Rose partnership was going, might be judged from a report submitted at a second meeting of the Court in March. Although the offer had been increased to 15 shillings in the pound no instalments had yet been paid. A promise was made to pay at least 2 shillings in the pound within a fortnight.[75]

The recovery of the debts then gathered pace. The sale of a Darlaston colliery had already been put in motion to realise £950.[76] In May 1858 an advert appeared for the sale of stock and effects at the Albert Ironworks which had been valued by the accountants at over £6,500, *'comprising 360 tons of pig iron, 150 tons of old castings, sixty tons of new ditto, eight tons of sheet bands, ten tons of sheet iron, two tons of new mill brasses, one ton of old ditto, twenty-six pair of forge, bar and sheet rolls, stock of merchant and use iron, fifteen tons of scrap iron, about four tons of floor plates, twenty tap wagons, thirty puddlers' boxes, four pig scales and weights, stamping press, set of circular shears, one 18 inch cylinder and nossel complete, 200 tons of calcined cinder, quantity of pinions, crabs and coupling boxes, forge and mill tools and trolleys, large smith's bellows, contents of blacksmith's shop, three tons of grease, lot of fire bricks, & c; also four iron open canal BOATS, six wood ditto, six useful waggon HORSES, gearing, six strong CARTS, four WAGGONS, built for the carriage of iron, strong four-wheel trolley, &c &c.'*[77]

It was a different case with the Eagle Ironworks. A further advert appeared later in the same month whereby its steam engine and all its puddling furnaces were offered for sale as well as the stock in hand.[78] These had been valued at £1300.

At the same time, Fletcher & Rose were desperately trying to recover monies owed to them. *The Birmingham Daily Post* carried an article on 21st July 1858 reporting on a dispute between the partnership and the Great Western Railway Company. The Birmingham, Wolverhampton and Dudley Railway ran over ground which was owned by Fletcher & Rose. Their mining operations, if continued, may have damaged the railway and the GWR initially offered to compensate Fletcher & Rose for not working the mine. There had been a debate over the amount to be paid. Fletcher & Rose claimed £412 which had been whittled down to £100. This amount had still not been paid since the rail company now claimed they were not liable to give compensation since they were entitled to construct supports for the track. The court found in favour of the rail company.[79]

What is remarkable about this is the fact that Fletcher & Rose were going through the courts to claim such a relatively small amount considering the scale of their debts. Even if they had been successful in this case it would have made little difference to their predicament.

What proved to be the saving of David Rose was the intervention of GB Thorneycroft, a Wolverhampton ironmaster. A private meeting of Fletcher & Rose's creditors was held in late July 1858 in which the inspectors reported that Thorneycroft had offered to purchase the Bradley colliery and its machinery paying: *'£26,000 down for the property, which will*

75. *The Birmingham Gazette*, 15th March 1858
76. *The Birmingham Daily Post*, 4th December 1857
77. *The Birmingham Gazette*, 3rd May 1858
78. *The Birmingham Gazette*, 17th May 1858
79. *The London Daily News*, 22nd July 1858 and *The Birmingham Daily Post*, 21st July 1858
80. *The Birmingham Daily Post*, 29th July 1858

enable Messrs Fletcher and Rose to pay 15s. in the pound, as agreed between them, and also give the firm possession of some £6,000, in addition.' [80]

Further pressure was levied on the company to pay 20 shillings in the pound but 15 shillings remained the amount.[81]

Rose, Higgins and Rose

While David was fighting to continue his business, his cousin Thomas had also been hit by the same financial crisis. Thomas Rose had ironworks and collieries in the Bilston area and employed around 300 men.[82]

The partnership of Rose, Higgins and Rose had been formed in 1849 to run the Bradleyfield Ironworks. Besides Thomas, the partnership included David and Daniel's brother, William, and Isaac Higgins. William left the business in 1853 and set up his own ironworks at Batman's Hill in Bilston. In June 1857 the partnership between Thomas Rose and Isaac Higgins was also dissolved, leaving Thomas in sole control.

This seems to have been a wise move for two of the partners for six months later in January 1858 the Birmingham Journal listed twenty-five firms which were in trouble. Rose, Higgins and Rose (the firm was still known as this despite the departure of two of the partners) owed £72,500 and had assets of only £29,417.[83] The anger expressed at how some ironmasters financed their works was again evident in the local press:

'They say their works cost them £25,000, so that giving them the utmost credit for their own statement, they advanced and spent £600 of their own money and £24,800 of other people's money and now they owe £72,500, besides their works.' [84]

An initial meeting of creditors pressed for the firm to be thrown into the Bankruptcy Court, but a second meeting, again chaired by Neil Solly, agreed that the works be carried on under inspection and, *'That Mr Rose shall pay a composition of 2s in the pound in three months; 2s in nine months; and further instalments at the rate of £5000 a year, until 10s in the pound in the whole shall have been paid.'* [85]

How the debts were paid off is clear from an advertisement in February 1858 for the sale of the Bradleyfield Ironworks which also gives us a detailed breakdown of what was on the site.

'They comprise three Condensing Engines, and one high-pressure Engine, with Boiler nearly new, and all in good working order, two Forges with thirty-two Puddling and Ball Furnaces, one Boiler-plate Mill, three Sheet Iron Mills, one Merchant Iron Mill and Guide Mill, Heating Furnaces, Warehouse, Shopping Foundry, Lathe, Pig Iron, Yard, Offices & c, and capable of turning out 180 to 200 tons of finished iron per week.' [86]

By September 1859 the debts had been cleared.[87] This was still a period of deep depression however. SH Blackwell wrote an assessment of the problems and prospects of

81. *The Birmingham Journal*, 31st July 1858
82. *The Worcestershire Chronicle*, 7th June 1854
83. Ray Shill, *South Staffordshire Ironmasters*, op.cit.
84. *The Birmingham Daily Post*, 22nd December 1857
85. *The Birmingham Daily Post*, 18th December 1857
86. *The Birmingham Gazette*, 22nd February 1858
87. *The Birmingham Journal*, September 1859

the Black Country's iron trade in the *Midlands Counties Herald* in June 1861. Many works were not only idle but would probably never work again, raw materials were difficult to obtain as the coal and iron fields had been largely mined out, mineral royalties were extortionate, wages too high and men were leaving for other districts where regular work could be obtained even though for low wages.

Blackwell, however, stressed that South Staffordshire was not finished, and listed its advantages – the ability to bring in ore and iron from elsewhere, its central position, high quality products and great local market. David Rose appears to have been one who, at least, for the next 15 years, saw ways to develop and prosper.

1836 picture of Bradley Ironworks, Robert Noyes, 1836.
(Courtesy Black Country Society Archive)

5. David Rose: recovery and expansion

Perhaps the key to David Rose's recovery was the dissolution of his partnership with Fletcher which was announced in December 1858: *'FLETCHER Richard Westley and David Rose, iron and coal masters, Moxley and Bradley, 16th Dec. Debts by Duignan & Ebsworth, solicitors, Walsall.'*[88]

While the Bradley Colliery and Eagle Ironworks had been sold off, David was still in possession of the Albert Works and he was able to begin to rebuild. During the early 1860s repayments to the Wolverhampton and Staffordshire Banking Company occurred on a regular basis and David not only began to consolidate, but also to expand his business.[89] The second half of the decade saw a spectacular growth in the firm as he took over the concerns of others who fell foul of downturns in the industry.

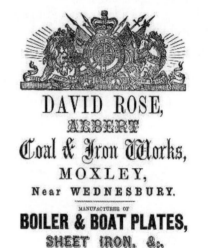

DAVID ROSE,
ALBERT
Coal & Iron Works,
MOXLEY,
Near WEDNESBURY.

MANUFACTURER OF

BOILER & BOAT PLATES,
SHEET IRON, &c.

SAND BEDS,
FIRE BRICK AND CLAY
WORKS.

An advert from 1861

The development of his business and his growth in stature is witnessed in several ways:

1. The continuation of his policy of obtaining small pieces of land to secure further supplies of ironstone and coal
2. His purchase of the Victoria Ironworks
3. The takeover of the Moxley Forge
4. The purchase of the Old Hill complex

Land purchases

During the 1860s David Rose pursued a policy of buying or leasing parcels of land to develop their underground minerals. He had taken out a lease on the Broadwater Colliery from Horace St. Paul in the late 1850s and did so again in 1861. A further lease agreement was signed in May 1873 with an annual rent of £10 per acre for the areas already broken. David also had to pay £200 per annum for coal, iron and limestone removed and was to give St Paul 30 tons of best coal annually. In addition he had to give any farming tenants one month's notice of his intention to sink any new shaft.[90]

In November 1861 he leased the rights to mines in Wednesbury from the trustees of the late Reverend John Holden. David was to pay them a seventh of the value of the thick coal mined plus 4d for every 22cwt of limestone and 1s 6d for every 1000 bricks or tiles made.[91]

88. *The Birmingham Gazette*, 25th December 1858
89. S.R.O. D1317/1/11/2/2
90. S.R.O.D1317/1/11/3/1
91. S.R.O. D1317/1/11/16/18

In December 1862 he leased Fiery Piece, Meadow Piece, Hilly Piece, The Mounts and Green Piece, which sat adjacent to the railway at Wednesbury, for 14 years.[92]

We also see how he did business with a family over several years. In September 1854 he had purchased a small strip of land from James Simkin. This was in Moxley and adjacent to Holyhead Road, the turnpike road from Bilston to Wednesbury. A plan shows that David Rose had a public house adjacent to Simkin's land. It was common for ironmasters to own public houses from which they regularly paid their workers' wages and thus more than likely benefitted from spending on beer. Simkin was the owner of the *Angel Inn* opposite Rose's own pub. When Simkin died in 1864 David Rose purchased the Angel, its brewhouse, outbuildings and land from his widow and her children for £518. It is clear, however, from the contract that David Rose intended to use the land for mining purposes.[93]

In July 1870 David Rose also bought 17 acres of land adjacent to Catherine's Cross in Darlaston. The areas consisted of Lower Crab Tree Piece, Crab Tree Piece, The Spigot and Forcet, The Slang and Flaunch Hole. The purchase included the mines beneath the land.[94] A further purchase included the Brickkiln Field and the Cow Fleet.[95] David's purchases were not restricted to the Darlaston, Wednesbury and Moxley areas. He also purchased mines under a piece of land called Homersfield at Mount Pleasant in Bilston.[96]

The purchases around the late 1860s and early 1870s coincided with the expansion of the Albert Iron Works and the construction of two blast furnaces. We do not know if all the coal from the Rose mines went to their ironworks. If it was sold on then the profits were indeed high. Barnsby has calculated that the profit margins were at least 250% in the boom years of the 1870s and 25% in the worst years of the depression.[97]

The purchase of the Victoria Ironworks

The iron industry in the early 1860s appeared to be in a settled state but it remained a volatile industry subject to highs and lows. When the next financial crisis hit in 1866 David was not a victim but one who benefitted from others misfortune. The panic had begun in May. In the previous month there had been concern over the prospect of war between Prussia and Austria. But the real trigger was the failure of the house of Overend and Gurney, standing second in prestige only to the Bank of England.

A general collapse followed and brought down many leading railway contractors. Ironmasters were forced to look at their profit margins and there was an obvious reaction from their workers. However, David Rose was now in a position to take advantage of the collapse in the market. The first purchase he made was that of the Victoria Ironworks in Moxley.

The Victoria Ironworks were run by Daniel Offley Senior, David's brother-in-law. David's son, Henry Fullwood Rose, at some point was in partnership with Daniel Offley. David Rose had become more of an astute businessman as a result of his experiences and may well have detected some weaknesses in his brother-in-law's business, passing on his

92. S.R.O. D13176/A/88/1
93. S.R.O D1317/1/11/7/1-7
94. S.R.O. D1317/1/11/16/18
95. S.R.O. D1317/1/11/3/1-17
96. S.R.O. D1317/1/11/1/3/1-17
97. George Barnsby, *'Social Conditions in the Black Country'*, 1980, p.241

advice to his son. In January 1865 Henry withdrew from the partnership.[98] Offley's firm also seemed to have additional problems. In April 1866 an advert had been placed warning businesses not to accept a bill of exchange from Samuel Chavasse, the firm's clerk, who had absconded with this and other monies.[99]

In August 1866 Daniel Offley and his sons Daniel and David were filed against for bankruptcy in connection with the Victoria Works, Moxley and the Grove Works, Smethwick. They had liabilities of £10,000 and assets of £3,000. They may well have overstretched themselves since they had only bought the Grove Works some two months earlier. The firm agreed to pay 4 shillings in the pound.[100]

The bankruptcy had dire consequences for the Offley family whose house contents were put up for sale in November of that year.[101] More importantly from a business perspective the contents of the Victoria Works were put up for sale in December 1866: *'consisting of two pair of new sheet Housings, 19 tons; capital Roll-turning Lathe, 6-horse power Engine, 50 pair Rolls, 60 tons Pig-Iron, 30 tons puddle Bars, 15 tons ball furnace Billets, Speedwheels and Arms, furnace Plates, Coupling Boxes, puddlers', furnace, mill, and blacksmith's Tools; Boxes, Spindles, Wheels, cinder Wagons, Boshes, Anvils, Bellows, hoop and round Iron, Grease, Oil, Scales, Weights, bundling Benches, quantity Coal, Horses, Wagons, Carts, Gearing & c & c together with seven capital open Boats ...'*[102]

There is no record of the purchaser but we can assume that David Rose took over the Victoria Works, with its eight puddling furnaces and two rolling mills, since he is listed as the owner in February 1868.[103]

The takeover of the Moxley Ironworks

The seriousness of the 1866 financial crisis was epitomised by the fortunes of Daniel Rose. For over 30 years Daniel had run a tight ship and had developed a profitable business but in February 1867 he had to suspend payments of bills. By this time Daniel was in his late 60s and the prospect of re starting his business was not one to contemplate. Daniel's partnership with Skidmore was dissolved in June 1867 with Skidmore picking up the debts.

In March 1867 Daniel handed control of all his other businesses to David, including all the fixed plant and machinery of the Moxley Ironworks. By this time the works had expanded considerably and by 1875 the site had ten puddling furnaces, three heating furnaces, an annealing furnace, a ball furnace, sheet mill, five beam engines and a wealth of other equipment housed in several buildings. (See Appendix 2)

David also picked up all the debts owed. The document outlining the terms of the transfer lists all the creditors, many of whom were central to the Black Country iron industry. Both men agreed to pay off the debts at 10 shillings for every pound in two instalments before September 1867. David also agreed to give his brother an annuity of £400.[104] The annuity was not required for long as Daniel died the following year in September 1868.

98. *Perry's Bankrupt Gazette*, 28th January 1865
99. *The Birmingham Daily Post*, 21st April 1866
100. *The Birmingham Journal*, 4th August 1866
101. *The Birmingham Daily Post*, 12th November 1866
102. *The Birmingham Journal*, 1st December 1866
103. List of the Mills and Forges in South Staffordshire, *The Birmingham Journal*, 29th February 1868
104. S.R.O. D1317/1/11/1/15/2

While David had taken over two of his relatives' ironworks, he did not, however, intervene in the demise of his cousin, Thomas Rose, whose Millfield Ironworks failed in June 1866 with liabilities of £40,000.[105]

The purchase of The Old Hill Works

The next major acquisition that David Rose made at this time was the Old Hill Furnaces, near Rowley Regis, which he purchased from Thomas & Isaac Badger. It was David's first attempt at integrating all the processes of iron manufacture since this site contained blast furnaces which his Moxley works lacked. The estate was advertised for sale in April 1868 with a detailed description of all its assets:

> 'containing together, about sixty acres; and the whole of the ungotten Mines of Brooch, Thick and Heathen Coals, Gubbin, and White Ironstone, lying in and under the same, of which a large quantity still remains in the solid and unworked.

> There are two Blast Furnaces upon the property, with ample engine power, Casting Houses, and the usual apparatus; the whole erected and made in the most costly manner; three pairs of Pit Shafts sunk down to the lower Mines, with three substantially erected Winding Engines, and apparatus complete; capital Manager's House, and numerous other Cottages for Workmen upon the Estate.

> The Property has every road, wharf and canal accommodation, with Tram and Railways already laid down to the canal and furnace bank, and is amply provided with Weighing Machines and everything necessary for the proper and efficient working of the Collieries and Furnaces, which for many years were so successfully carried on by the late Messrs. Badger.'[106]

David Rose's purchase of the site for a mere £17,500 was reported later in the month – the unfavourable state of the iron trade being perceived as the main reason for the low price.[107] Even so, the report of the outlay would have made interesting reading to the creditors of Daniel Rose who had been paid off at 10 shillings in the pound a year earlier.

It is also clear that the purchase signalled some hope for the ironworkers and colliers of the district and, indeed, within a short time the works were employing 60 to 80 men.[108]

The progress of the works can also be seen from a letter written by David Rose to his daughter-in-law Lydia, the wife of William Napoleon Rose, circa 1868, David says: *'Tell Will we are going on very well at Old Hill and we hope by the time we come back we shall be sending coal to the works.'*[109]

Ewart Chapman's painting of the Old Hill Ironworks. (Courtesy Dudley Archives & Local History Service)

105. *The Birmingham Journal*, 22nd June 1866
106. *Aris's Birmingham Gazette*, 4th April 1868
107. *The Birmingham Daily Post*, 29th April 1868
108. Parliamentary Papers 1871: A Report on the Truck System. Part 2, Special reports p.693
109. Wolverhampton Archives, DX-219/10

(Right) Letter from David Rose to his daughter-in-law, Lydia, updating her on the progress of the Old Hill Works.
(Courtesy Wolverhampton Archives Services).

The Old Hill Blast Furnaces appear to have been slow to develop. A list of furnaces in the area, in 1869, shows that neither of the Old Hill ones was in blast.[110] However, by early 1870 progress was being made. It was reported that: *'The Coal trade of South Staffordshire continues steady, and prices are well maintained ... The Pig-iron trade is well sustained, best brand especially maintaining the improvement noticed a few weeks ago. Another furnace has been blown in this week at Red Hill (sic) by Mr David Rose. It is constructed on the improved plan lately adopted in this district for economising fuel and utilising the waste gases.'*[111]

Blast furnace records show that only one of the two furnaces at Old Hill was in blast during David Rose's tenure.[112] After his new blast furnaces were constructed at Moxley, David Rose sold the Old Hill works to Noah Hingley in 1872.

How his fortunes had changed is evident from their taking responsibility for overseeing the administration of other struggling firms. In March 1867 he was appointed a trustee to assist with the payment of the creditors of S Carter, an iron girder manufacturer, of King's Hill in Wednesbury.[113] When the firm of Harbord, Wilkinson and Co. failed in 1870, a committee of inspection was set up, comprising a number of creditors, to advise on the administration of the estate. William Rose, David's son, was one of those appointed.[114]

110. *The Birmingham Daily Post*, 8th April 1869
111. *The Birmingham Daily Post*, 5th February 1870
112. P Riden, *'British Blast Furnace Statistics, 1790 -1980'*, 1995. p.79
113. *The Birmingham Journal*, 9th March 1867
114. *The London Standard*, 7th October 1870

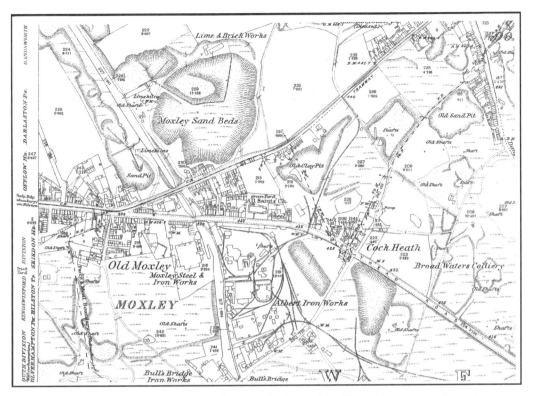

Map of Moxley in the late 19th century showing the Albert Iron Works, Broadwater(s) Colliery and the Moxley sand beds.

6. The growth of the Albert and Victoria Works: galvanising and the introduction of blast furnaces at Moxley: 1868-1873

Iron prices were rising in the late 1860s and this was directly linked to the demand for coal. David Rose had his own collieries which supplied his works but down to 1871 the coal industry had been starved of profits for several years. This soon changed and the price of coal in London reached an extraordinary level of over 50 shillings a ton. Another factor in the rise in the price of iron was the onset of the Franco-Prussian War which meant that two large states partially suspended production. At the end of 1871 the price of bar iron began to climb from an average of £8 per ton to around £16 in July 1872. Output struggled to keep up with demand despite the fact that 1871 saw production of pig iron in the Black Country reach a near peak of over 725,000 tons. This was to be the last big wave of prosperity in the Midland iron industry before its eclipse by steel.

Consequently, around the late 1860s and the beginning of the 1870s, there was an expansion at the Victoria & Albert Works. Both works were already quite large - the Albert Works had 15 puddling furnaces and 3 rolling mills while the Victoria Works had 8 puddling furnaces and 2 rolling mills.[115] An indication of the speed of the expansion may be gleaned from the fact that by 1873 the Albert Works had 22 puddling furnaces.[116] By 1871 David Rose's Moxley works, including ironworks and coal mines, employed 458 people.[117]

Newspaper adverts featuring the Albert Works in this period bear witness to the constant demand for both equipment and workers. Equipment was sought in the form of *'a good Second-hand PUNCHING MACHINE, suitable for punching plates.'*[118] *'A High-pressure Beam or Vertical STEAM ENGINE, Cylinder 20 inches, Stroke 3 feet or 3 feet 6 inches.'*[119] *'A Second-hand Vertical DRILLING MACHINE, with Back Gear, capable of drilling a two-inch hole.'*[120] *'Ten Tons of Second- hand T.RAILS about 40lbs per yard.'*[121] and *'125 yards of 14in. or 15.in. Socket or Flange PIPES. New or Second-hand.'*[122]

The recruitment drive included adverts for a 'forge and mill manager'[123], a 'millwright'[124] and 'foreman boiler maker'.[125]

Galvanising

David Rose also developed a galvanising plant at the Albert Works in this period, as did his brother William at the Batman's Hill Works. Warren gives the background to the emergence of galvanising in the Black Country in this period.[126]

115. List of Mills and Forges, 1868. op. cit.
116. *Griffiths Guide to the Iron Trade*, 1873, p.269
117. Report on the Truck System. op. cit.
118. *The Birmingham Daily Post*, 17th June 1868
119. *The Birmingham Daily Post*, 3rd May 1869
120. *The Birmingham Daily Gazette*, 11th May 1869
121. *The Birmingham Daily Post*, 25th April 1871
122. *The Birmingham Daily Post*, 21st September 1871
123. *The Birmingham Daily Post*, 11th August 1868
124. *The Birmingham Daily Post*, 29th July 1869
125. *The Birmingham Daily Post*, 11th July 1870
126. K Warren, *The British Iron and Steel Sheet Industry since 1840*, 1970, Pp 13-25

While rising material costs had priced the Black Country out of the rail trade, the wider margins found in quality products had increasingly attracted some ironmasters' attention to them. One of these products was sheet iron. Sheets were rolled from puddled iron bars in rolling mills, known as two-high mills. Like a mangle, they could be adjusted to produce the desired thickness. Standard thickness gauges were introduced in the 1880s. The process often required several passes and re-heatings so proximity to low cost coal supplies was desirable. The iron also had to be of high quality to undergo repeated working.

One of the problems with producing sheet iron had been its susceptibility to weathering. It was then that a practical galvanising process was introduced, with powdered or molten zinc, with the result of a large increase in demand. Galvanising required good quality sheet which retained its malleability when dipped into molten zinc. In October 1866 the journal Engineer explained the process. Piles of black sheet iron were first pickled in tanks of sulphuric acid to clean them, then washed, scraped, dipped in hydrochloric acid, washed again and dried. Using tongs, they were then slipped into a bath full of molten spelter surrounded by a coke fire. The sheets were then pulled out of the other side by men who checked that the zinc had taken. The process might well explain why, as we shall see, there were complaints from the local neighbourhood about David Rose's works.

While production of black sheets required a lot of coal and good quality iron, galvanising used little coal and quickly developed a large export market. The trade in galvanised sheet iron expanded in the 1870s amidst the decline in other areas of the industry. It also required a suitably skilled workforce which is manifested by the adverts which appeared on a frequent basis in the *Birmingham Daily Post* with Rose's Albert Works seeking, amongst others, a corrugator and a set of galvanisers who needed to be 'steady men', an experienced sheet iron roller, a 'steady, competent strip roller' and a foreman with a knowledge of galvanising.[127]

Galvanising proved to be one of David Rose's most profitable operations in the late 1860s and 1870s. While some iron manufacturing processes were in decline, galvanising plants and rolling mills reached their peak in 1882.[128]

Blast furnaces at the Albert Works
At this time David Rose and his sons made several visits with various institutes to look at emerging technology. One of these was to the North East to inspect blast furnaces. The result of this endeavour became clear in a report which appeared in June 1870: *'Messrs Rose, of the Albert Works, Moxley, will begin a new furnace, which is to be furnished with all the modern appliances for the economising of fuel and augmenting heat, which is, in fact, to be similar to the furnaces which have been worked with such satisfactory results in the Middlesboro district. The South Staffordshire ironmasters have been slow to adopt the new furnaces, and to this, many persons versed in such matters, attribute the backward position of the trade in the district. Messrs Rose intend in a few weeks to erect a second furnace on the same principle in another part of their premises.'*[129]

These developments again led to a flurry of adverts requiring an engineer to remove and re-erect a blast engine as well as a stock-taker[130] - a vital role in the measuring out of the

127. *The Birmingham Daily Post*, 18th February 1870, 19th June 1971, 10th August 1872, 1st July 1874
128. Gale, *'The Black Country Iron Industry'*, op. cit. p.105
129. *The London Standard*, 3rd June 1870
130. *The Birmingham Daily Post*, 11th July 1870, 30th September 1870

raw materials to be mixed in the blast furnace. All this activity came to fruition in December 1871 when David's daughter Elizabeth officially opened the Prince of Wales Furnaces at Moxley, described as: *'almost a model plant in Staffordshire, where they are the newest completed. They are very large, and have been built entirely upon modern principles, including the drawing down of the gases to the boilers, blast stoves, calcining kilns and the like.'* [131]

We can assume from this that the furnaces incorporated Cowper stoves which worked on a regenerative principle. Hot gases from the blast furnace were drawn through one stove in order to heat the brick. Then air for the blast was blown through the stove while the waste heat from the furnace was directed through a second stove.

The 1862 Children's Employment Commission, reporting on the ironworks of South Staffordshire, indicates that the average number of men employed at furnaces was around 24, if there were both day and night shifts, but we do not know if this was the modus operandi at the Moxley Works. The Commission's report includes a graphic description of both the processes involved and the working conditions of the blast furnaces at Lloyds, Foster & Co in Wednesbury which were just a mile or so from David Rose's Albert Works:

> *'We cross to the three tall blazing furnaces: in the rear boys are breaking up the limestone into small lumps, under a range of sheds, and men are filling enormous wheel-barrows with the roasted ore, with coal and coke, and the broken limestone. From the sheds a broad incline extends to the top of the furnaces, and up this the barrows are wheeled and placed one behind the other in a certain order, and the machinery being set at work, they are hauled up one side of the slope, while a train of empty barrows descends on the other.*
>
> *We walk up and find ourselves on an iron platform, forty feet from the ground, and so near to the blazing crests of the three furnaces as to induce a moment's pause. The heat, however, is bearable, and we can walk round the craters, as they may be called, and look down upon the preparations in the foundry beneath, and listen to the roar with wonder. But the barrows are up: the 'filler' opens an iron door, wheels the foremost barrow across the platform, and shoots its load of half-a-ton into the furnace; then another, and another till they are emptied, when they are sent down to be refilled and more full ones are drawn up. The opening of the door makes us start back from the intolerable heat and glare for there we look directly into the furnace, on a level with the summit of a huge mass of fire, forty feet in height. We can almost fancy it a volcano, so fierce is the heat, so angry the roar; and we are impressed beyond previous conception by the tremendous forces required to make nature surrender her mineral treasures ...*
>
> *We walk ... round the base of the furnaces and see how they are ribbed and hoped with iron to support the massive brick walls. A fierce glow shows under the vent; from time to time a molten stream, white hot, flows down the heap of ashes and clinkers, and solidifies in those strange looking masses of slag ... From time to time the chain is lowered, and the ponderous discs are hauled up an incline and dragged away to widen the enormous refuse heaps which encumber the ground ...*

131. *The Engineer*, December 29th, P.434

On the low earthen floors in front of the furnaces men are busy laying down solid beds of sand, and forming therein a series of gutters, of which those running lengthwise are as broad and deep again as those crossing at right angles. ... The foundry men wait expectant, having prepared all their moulds, the huge ladle is lowered into its pit, and the keepers are listening for the signal word. It is spoken. The one nearest the furnace makes a few heavy lunges with a long bar at the clay which stops the tapping-hole, lump after lump falls away, a sudden twinkle appears and out rushes the molten iron, and flows rapidly down the sloping channel to the pit, where it shoots a cascade of fire, into the huge pot. Turn aside, or shut your eyes, and you may fancy that cream is pouring out, so liquid is the sound of glowing metal. The stream ripples as it flows up brilliant coruscations at the plunge. Presently a shout announces that the pot is full; at once the stream is diverted into a side channel; on it flows, glowing and quivering, and forthwith all the cross gutters are filled, and from the appearances you might fancy the large sand-bed covered by a red-hot grid-iron. ..

And the while we see a sight that makes us think of walking on red-hot plough-shares with diminished admiration, for the men, indifferent alike, as it seems to the sulphurous fumes and red-hot iron, walk up and down the ranges of bars, spade in hand, and cover them with sand, exclusion of air being desirable during the cooling. In the grid-irons, as we have called them, the principal channel is called the 'sow'; the minor lateral channels are the 'pigs'. Hence the term 'pig-iron.' [132]

Pig beds at a blast furnace. (From a postcard in the author's collection)

132. W White, *'All around the Wrekin'*, 1860, pp.271-280

Ede states that the Albert Works furnaces were capable of producing 20,000 tons of pig-iron annually and that: *'David Rose & Co. thus exemplified what was becoming a characteristic feature of the iron trade, its integration under a single management of all the successive processes of iron manufacture – mining, both of coal and iron, smelting, puddling and rolling.'* [133]

The scope of the works is clear from an advert in Samuel Griffiths' *Guide to the Iron Trade*, published in 1873.

DAVID ROSE,
IRONMASTER,
THE
ALBERT & MOXLEY IRONWORKS,
MOXLEY
(Also The MOXLEY BLAST FURNACES),

MANUFACTURES

BEST AND BEST-BEST-BEST

BOILER PLATES,

SHEET-IRON OF ALL KINDS,

INCLUDING

GASOMETER SHEETS, SHEETS FOR GALVANIZERS

AND CORRUGATING,

RUSSIAN ROOFING SHEETS.

GALVANISING.

SUGAR-MOULDS FOR TINNING,

PAN AND TANK PLATES,

ALL KINDS OF BARS,

Small Rounds and Squares and Fancy Iron.

ALSO,

GALVANISING SHEETS
made at the Works, where both Galvanising and Corrugating
are carried on on a large scale.

PIG IRON
is also made at the Blast Furnaces, and

FIRE BRICKS
for Sale in the district.

POSTAL ADDRESS:—
DAVID ROSE,
MOXLEY.

Advert in Samuel Griffiths' Guide to the Iron Trade, 1873

These developments marked the height of David Rose's success as an industrialist – but the seeds of decline were already sown. Pig iron production in the Black Country had reached its peak in 1863.[134] Records show that the only time both of Rose's blast furnaces were in operation was in 1879. Indeed, between 1876 and 1878, both were idle. After 1879 neither of them was ever used.[135]

133. JF Ede, *'History of Wednesbury'*, 1962, p. 268
134. Gale, op.cit. p.105
135. Riden, op.cit. p.76

7. The challenges of securing supplies: coal and iron ore

We have seen how David Rose owned or leased a number of collieries in an attempt to be as self-sufficient as possible as far as raw materials for iron production were concerned. Apart from the purchases of many small plots of land for their mineral rights, there are references to the Broadwater Colliery, the Albert Colliery, the Waterloo Colliery and the Woods Bank Colliery, as well as the mines at Old Hill and his brief tenure of the Bradley Colliery. He is also recorded as the part-owner of the Rough Hay Colliery in 1884.

South Staffordshire was fortunate to have a uniquely rich bed of coal known as the 'Ten Yard Seam'. Nowhere else in Britain had coal of such quality and quantity at a relatively shallow depth and references to the coal seam at Moxley go back many years. Annual output in South Staffordshire peaked in 1865 with some 400 collieries producing around 400 million tons of coal. This was about 40% of the national total. Most of the operations were quite small. In 1874 37,000 miners were employed at 469 collieries, an average of less than 80 men to each colliery of several pits[136]. David Rose's pits epitomised this method of operating.

A pithead at Moxley in the late 19th century.
(Courtesy Dudley Archives & Local History Service)

The 1st Report of the Midland Mining Commission in 1843 described that a typical Wednesbury pit of the time consisted of 15 or 16 men, two women and about half a dozen boys. Pikemen hewed the coal while bandsmen loaded and hoisted the skips, assisted by both women and children[137].

136. *Barnsby, op.cit. p.24*
137. *Parliamentary Papers, First Report of the Midland Mining Commission, 1843*

Mine owners like David Rose tended to operate at arm's length from day to day operations, leaving a chartermaster, known as a 'butty', acting as a middleman. Butties were paid by the ton. Expected yield and the price per ton for various grades of coal were specified. So with regards to the daily man management of his pits, David had few problems. The problems posed by miners' strikes will be examined in a later chapter. By far the biggest physical challenge posed to coal mining in South Staffordshire was flooding.

In 1870 it was calculated that 150 million tons of coal and 20 million tons of ironstone were under water in South Staffordshire. The larger owners employed pumping engines and often found themselves draining their neighbours' pits at their own expense and, in any case, when the water raised was run into streams, much of it percolated back into the mines. Ownership or tenancy of his mines involved David Rose in two legal cases in which drainage problems were to the fore.

Roberts and Yardley v Rose

The first of these concerned the Albert and Broadwater Collieries. The case was first heard at the Staffordshire Assizes in spring 1864 before being later heard in the House of Lords. Roberts was the plaintiff and Rose the defendant. It concerned a watercourse being blocked which led to the flooding of Roberts' Bank Mine. David Rose had initially allowed the watercourse to be constructed by Roberts on his own land where it emptied itself into an old excavation of his Broadwater Colliery.

The case reveals that David Rose had leased the Broadwater Colliery from Sir Horace St Paul in 1861 to mine the remaining coal, ironstone and clay. The lease gave David Rose permission to construct roads, railways, cuts, canals, wharfs, landing places, yards, basins, drains and watercourses on the land. David Rose was also the lessee of the Albert Colliery and raised coal from the Broadwater Colliery up the shafts of the Albert Colliery, making a cut from this colliery to the watercourse.

In March 1862 David Rose objected to the use of the watercourse by Roberts and applied for a money payment to be paid for the use of the watercourse. Rose said that the watercourse was badly kept and damaging his own mining operations. He therefore blocked the watercourse but without obstructing the flow of water from the Albert Colliery which was downstream from the blockage!

The Bank Colliery was damaged by the subsequent flooding and Roberts objected that the blockage could have been done elsewhere and a drain constructed to prevent damage to anyone's mines. After lengthy deliberations David Rose won the case, although there must have been considerable bad feeling afterwards between David Rose and his neighbours[138].

If as much money, care and attention had been paid to the workings of the mine as was paid to the court case, then the accidents that occurred at these pits, which we will cover later, might have been prevented.

It is no surprise that the Broadwater Colliery was subject to flooding. The very name might be a bit of a giveaway. Hackwood, writing in 1899, mentions that at one time the area *was the resort of vast numbers of waterfowl; in old times the heron and the bittern*

---

138. *The Staffordshire Advertiser*, 19th March & 7th May 1864;. House of Lords Reports V. 159, 1864 p.95

made their homes on its banks. Within the memory of at least one old inhabitant wild-duck shooting had been enjoyed there.' [139]

The Old Hill Colliery: Rose v Pearson

The second case concerned David Rose and the coalmasters at Old Hill. Initially David Rose and the firms of Hingley, J&W Pearson, Mills and Nock met in February 1870 to consider how they might tackle the problem of flooding and, *'after discussing the subject at some length, they resolved themselves into an association, and subscribed funds to start the Windmill End pumping engine, and the New Buffery pumping engine.'* [140]

This show of unity did not last long since a dispute soon arose between David Rose and J and W Pearson whose collieries adjoined each other. The Pearsons took David Rose to court since he, *'finding his workings impeded by the water which lay in them, cut a road or water level to within a few yards of his boundary, adjoining the plaintiffs' and let the water down the road; and as no rib existed, the water went through the old workings into the plaintiffs' colliery, and so did them considerable damage.'* [141]

David Rose argued that he had a perfect right to cut a road to channel water from this mine and that it was the Pearsons' fault from not having constructed a barrier to protect their property. The case was postponed while both sides gathered evidence but in the meantime David Rose was allowed to channel off water. The issue appears to have been resolved because there was no further coverage of the case. Whatever the solution in this case, moves were afoot to try and tackle the issue of flooding on a wider basis.

The South Staffordshire Mines Drainage Act

A petition to Parliament by local coalmasters led to the South Staffordshire Mines Drainage Act of 1873. This created a Board of Commissioners empowered to install pumping machinery and to levy a flat rate per ton on all coal, slack and fireclay raised. The whole of the area was divided into 5 districts for pumping operations, one of which covered the mines around Bilston.

However, there were objections from mine owners such as David Rose which were raised at a public meeting called by the South Staffordshire Mines Drainage Commissioners to hear appeals.[142] Their objections centred around the proposal for charging a uniform rate on each ton of minerals raised, and many argued that the rate should be graduated. Several other firms testified that they had not benefitted from the Commission's pumping engines. After much deliberation, David Rose's mines were declared exempt from the uniform rate, together with those of the Darlaston Steel and Iron Company and the Patent Shaft and Axletree Company. Other companies had their appeals rejected or their rates reduced. Grumbles continued into 1876. Many companies complained that several of the Commission's pumps had stopped some time previously but water levels had not really risen and a petition was drawn up against the rate.[143]

The coalmasters may have been correct in their opinions about the effectiveness of pumping machinery. In 1877 Messrs Groucutt of Moxley closed down their collieries at

139. FW Hackwood: *'Olden Wednesbury: its whims and ways'*, p.34
140. *The Birmingham Daily Post*, 14th February 1870
141. *The Birmingham Daily Post*, 26th May 1871
142. *The Birmingham Daily Post*, 10th August 1875
143. *The Birmingham Gazette*, 30th December 1876

Bilston and Moxley where rising water had 'overcome the pumps.'[144] David Rose's Moxley mines were also affected since it was reported in May 1884 that the Broadwater Colliery had been drowned out for seven years.[145] Despite this, in 1878 greater powers of raising money were granted to the Board of Commissioners and in the next 10 years £100,000 was spent on pumping the deeper workings with rates being raised on tonnage.

The Deepfields drainer: one of the pumping stations of the South Staffordshire Drainage Commission.   *(Courtesy Wolverhampton Archives Services)*

Securing iron ore and coal supplies from further afield

While coal was available from David Rose's own pits, the supply of iron ore to feed his blast furnaces was another matter. The reserves of ironstone in the Black Country were not inexhaustible. As early as the mid-1840s Gibbons' Corbyn Hall furnaces were securing iron stone from Lancashire and Coventry[146] and the quarterly meeting of the Staffordshire and Shropshire ironmasters in April 1854 focussed on the dearth of ironstone.[147] Blackwell calculated that the rising price of raw materials was drastically reducing the profit margins for producing affordable pig iron in Staffordshire.[148]

By 1870 most of the iron ore resources in the Black Country had been worked out and ironmasters had to look further afield. One example of how David Rose tried to secure his

144. *The Edinburgh Evening News*, 29th May 1877
145. *The Birmingham daily Post,* 26th May 1884
146. Birch, op.cit. p.154
147. H Scrivenor, *'The History of the Iron Trade'* p.299
148. Blackwell, *'The Iron-making Resources of the United Kingdom'* 1852, quoted by Scrivenor op.cit. pp.300-301

supplies comes from his correspondence in 1875 with the Wyken Colliery Company near Coventry.[149] The South Midlands Mining, Civil and Mechanical Engineers, of which David Rose was a member, had visited the Warwickshire coalfield in August 1873 when a paper had been read mentioning Wyken and its ironstone deposits.[150] The group also descended one of the ironstone pits in the area. It is highly likely that one of the Rose family was a member of this party.

Letter to Charles Ryland, concerning Wyken Colliery. (Courtesy Waterways Archive)

David's first correspondence concerning the Wyken Colliery was in February 1875 with a letter addressed to Charles Ryland, a Birmingham iron merchant and, who was, on occasions, the middle man between the Roses and the Wyken Colliery.

'Dear Sirs
Please order forwarded to my works per London & North Western 50 tons of Black Ironstone at 18/- per ton and as I am short of trucks please ask The Wyken Co to deliver charging freight & truck hire.

Yours Truly
David Rose
Per W.N. Rose'

P.S. This as sample to be increased if I approve of the quality.'

149. The Waterways Archive, BW83/14/1/1/12
150. *The Leamington Spa Courier*, 23rd August 1873
151. The Waterways Archive BW83

38

Ten days later David Rose returned a signed contract to the Wyken Colliery ordering 500 lots of: *'Black Stone or any portion of White'* to be delivered weekly by rail in 50 or 60 ton lots.

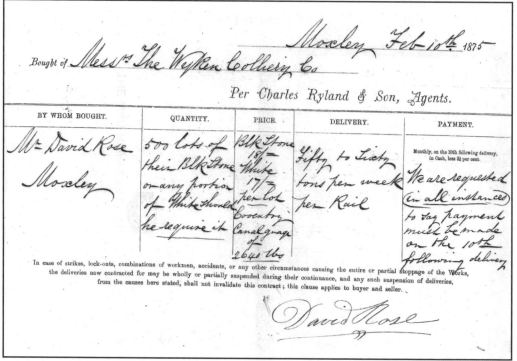

Order from David Rose to Wyken Colliery. (Courtesy of the Waterways Archive)[152]

On April 1st another note revealed the businessman in David Rose:

'Dear Sirs

I am surprised to hear The Railway Co. have advanced their rate to my Works and I trust you may be able to get it delivered at former rate. I may inform you that I have an offer before me at 1/- per ton less for Ironstone from your district. I should prefer doing business with you now we have fairly commenced and shall be pleased to hear you can meet me in the price. In any case send on a supply of Ironstone.'

A further request was sent by postcard 3 days later. On May 7th David Rose sent a note indicating that he had not received the shipment that had been promised. Further correspondence in September requested the lowest prices for Wyken ironstone but they were *'not in a position to supply.'* However an invoice on December 4th from Ryland indicates they had sent another 50 tons. This is the last correspondence.

David Rose also sourced ironstone from Derbyshire, evidenced by a report of a case in the Court of Appeal concerning an unfulfilled contract. In August 1878 the Ainsworth Iron Company of Ilkeston had agreed to supply 500 tons of grey forge iron at £2 10s a ton, to be delivered in parcels of 100 tons monthly. However when the market was falling, the deliveries were suspended at the Rose company's request. When the price of iron rose in

152. Ibid

39

December 1879, David Rose demanded the completion of the contract. The Ainsworth Iron Company contended that the contract time had expired and that they were unable to supply the outstanding 322 tons. They also refused to pay compensation demanded at £3 15s per ton. Hence the court action.[153]

We also know from a list of creditors drawn up when Daniel handed over his concerns to David that he too had been sourcing ironstone from other areas. One of the creditors was the West Cumberland Haematite Company.[154] The competitiveness of their rates was plain to see. Blackwell had calculated that the cost of mining these ores was under 2s 6d per ton compared to 4s 9d for local ironstone.[155]

It is clear that David Rose was a man who had done his research and was extremely knowledgeable about local coal and iron mines. A note in the flyleaf of a book borrowed from his library reads, *'Some account of the Coalmines and Ironstone Mines at Chorley in the parish of Stottesden and in the neighbourhood thereof. Collected from the best accounts that could be obtained and from thirty years observation by Thomas Crump of Chorley, 1799. Copy of an old ms. in the possession of the Rev. Dupre, Rector of Highley. Lent me (Daniel Jones) by Mr David Rose, Goldthorn Court, Wolverhampton, April 4th 1874. '*[156]

Similarly, David's cousin, Thomas Rose, who had also recovered from his bankruptcy in the late 1850s, was attempting to expand his source of raw materials. There are records of three companies that he was involved in which were bringing in raw materials from further afield. First, in February 1864 he was named as one of the directors of the newly formed North Stafford Steel, Iron and Coal Company which was, *'formed to develop two rich virgin mineral properties in North Staffordshire viz, 'The Rushton Grange' and 'Dog Croft' Estates held under leases from Lord Camoys and W. Heath Esq, respectively, and for the manufacture of Bessemer Steel and Finished Iron.*

The Ironstone, computed to yield 20,000,000 tons can be cheaply worked. The analyses of Dr Percy F.R.S. show 39% iron. The Coal varies from 2 feet 6 to 10 feet 6 in thickness, and gives a total of 50,000,000 tons, adapted for pottery and domestic use, and there is a valuable deposit of superior Fire-clay...'[157]

In addition to this, Thomas Rose was sourcing coal from two mines in Wales where he was one of the partners in the Little Mountain Coal and Cannel Company in Buckley, along with Joseph Turner, the colliery manager, and John Postlethwaite.[158] Thomas was also one of nine directors of the Mold Consolidated Lead Mining Company formed in July 1865 *'to reopen and work the celebrated Cat Hole and Gwern-y-Mynydd Mines of Lead and Zinc Ores, situate in the parish of Mold, in the county of Flint. The Sett is very extensive, including about 300 acres, and is held upon a highly favourable lease ... for a term of twenty-one years, at a royalty of one-fifteenth for the first half of the term and one-twelfth for the remaining half ...'*[159]

153. *The Nottingham Evening Post*, 19th June 1882
154. S.R.O. D1317/1/11/1/15/2
155. Blackwell, op.cit.
156. Notebook in the library of the British Geological Survey
157. *The Liverpool Daily Post*, 10th February 1864
158. *The London Gazette*, June 6th 1865
159. *The Birmingham Journal*, 22nd July 1865

Securing supplies also meant looking at transport networks. Care had been taken to site the Moxley and Albert Ironworks adjacent to the Birmingham Canal. The canal network was important in both transporting raw materials and finished goods. The list of Daniel Rose's creditors in 1867 includes the Birmingham Canal Company as well as the Shropshire Union Canal Company.[160] The Roses were also involved in lobbying for an extension to the Gloucester and Berkeley Canal in 1870. Henry Fullwood Rose gave evidence before a committee of the House of Lords regarding a bill in favour of the extension. *'The evidence of Mr Rose and Mr Gibbs went to show that the proposed extension would be of great advantage to the South Staffordshire iron trade, particularly in consequence of the reduced rates. They showed that the present rates to Liverpool were 11s per ton, and said the saving would be 4s to 5s per ton in favour of Gloucester if that were made the port for South Staffordshire.'*[161]

Sometimes these transport links broke down. In January 1871, the bed of the Birmingham Canal at Moxley collapsed due to mining works.[162] David Rose's operations would have been affected on several counts – possible damage to his mines and loss of raw materials for his newly constructed blast furnaces as well as delays in delivering finished products. The following week another problem developed when it was reported that, *'Business at the works is still much impeded by the large quantity of floating ice in the canals.'*[163]

David Rose also took advantage of the development of the rail network as we have seen from his correspondence with the Wyken Colliery. With the construction of the blast furnaces at the Albert Works there was a need for a way to deliver raw materials in bulk but also with speed. In 1872 the local board gave permission for David to lay a railway track from the Albert Works connecting them with the Darlaston branch of the London and North Western Railway near Wednesbury, at a point which became known as Roses Sidings.[164]

The Rose concerns were not only dependent on transport networks - the networks that they created with other iron and coal masters were just as important for the long term prosperity of the business.

160. S.R.O. D1317/1/11/15/2
161. *Aris's Birmingham Gazette,* 18th September 1869
162. *The Salisbury and Winchester Journal,* 21st January 1871
163. *The Leeds Mercury,* 27th January 1871
164. R Shill, *'Industrial Locomotives of the West Midlands,'* 1992, p.146

8. Ironmaster networks

How ironmasters controlled the market

Quarterly meetings of the Midlands ironmasters were held in Wolverhampton at the Old Exchange. This practice had been established in the early 1800s and continued until the 1870s. Ironmasters used the meeting to request payments and receive orders and the system allowed an ironworks to organise its production over a three-month period. It also informed ironmasters what grades and types of iron were in demand, and presented choices to them of either producing a variety of special products, or risking production on fewer, more regular types of bar iron in the hope that the price would remain profitable.

By taking orders at quarterly intervals, ironmasters could ensure that no iron was left unsold. Business was organised in such a way that the finished product was in circulation for as short a time as possible. Prices of iron and coal were fixed at quarterly meetings. Since few of the major ironworks kept significant stocks of iron, it was permanently in their interest to keep the price of iron as profitable as possible.

Quarter days were also a social occasion. Such contacts were also useful when ironmasters needed to unite in defence of their interests or broker partnerships. We can assume all the Rose brothers attended these meetings but the only specific mention of the family comes in January 1874 when David's son, Henry is reported as attending.[165]

Not only could they control prices but the ironmasters could also control wages. This applies to coal mining too – most ironmasters were coal-masters and there was also a coal-masters association. As Barnsby notes, this was less blatant but the evidence shows that in the disputes of 1864 and 1874 the employers negotiated together.[166]

Ironmasters were also struggling to achieve some commonality in standard gauges for their sheet iron to help market their wares. As Gale notes, the situation was chaotic. There were several gauges and the usual standard in the Black Country for sheets and hoops was the Birmingham Gauge. *'This might appear simple enough, until it was realised that there was no general agreement as to what B.G. really was… The position was not improved by the fact that manufacturers in the Black Country offered for sale sheets and other products in gauge sizes without specifying what gauge they meant.'*[167]

In 1858 James Rose, son of William and nephew of David and Daniel attempted to rectify the problem by publishing *'A New Guide to the Iron Trade'*, which contained a set of tables to show the weight of iron required to produce boiler plates, sheet iron as well as hoop and strip iron. The tables attempted to make a comparison with known gauges. However, the situation remained confused until early in the 20th century.

'Mining' and sharing information: How David Rose kept informed

Besides the iron and coal-master meetings there was another network in the form of the many institutes which sprang up in the Black Country in the mid-nineteenth century to encourage the dissemination of the latest engineering knowledge. The Rose family were members of several of these.

165. *Birmingham Daily Post*, 5th January 1874
166. Barnsby, op. cit. p.45
167. Gale, op.cit. p.96

The national organisation of the Institute of Mining Engineers had been founded in 1867. The president and guiding spirit was Henry Johnson who in 1864 said that education, kind treatment and high wages were the greatest evils to the collier! David Rose attended a Coal Trade dinner in Middlesbrough in May 1869[168] which was part of a two day visit to the North East by the Staffordshire and Worcestershire Institute of Mining Engineers. It was a very full schedule. On the first day, the party visited the Acklam, Middlesbrough and Linthorpe Ironworks where they viewed blast furnaces and rolling mills. This was followed by a trip to Backhouse & Dixon's iron shipbuilding yard. The party also inspected the ironworks of Bolckow, Vaughan & Co at Eaton Junction, one of the largest ironworks in the country, as well as visiting their coal and ironstone mines. This was at the time when David Rose was embarking on the construction of his own blast furnaces at Moxley so he may well have been picking up useful tips.

How much these men were in touch with the day to day experiences of mining operations may be judged from the report of their underground experience. *'Trudging for miles upon a narrow railway ... the party were anxious to reach day-light, and shortly afterwards, when the cage brought them to bank, they indulged in mutual congratulations that they had passed through so much in safety.'*[169]

The following day the party visited Ryhope Colliery, near Sunderland. The same colliery received another visit in August that year, this time on the occasion of the annual meeting of the National Institute of Mechanical Engineers which took place at Newcastle.Again, a Mr Rose of Wednesbury is listed as being in attendance together with several Midlands Ironmasters, including George Addenbrooke of Darlaston. Addenbrooke addressed the meeting stressing the necessity of close co-operation: *'now these foreign nations had learned a deal, and were enabled to turn out good workmen in opposition to them, so that unless the English engineers kept together in scientific work, they must undoubtedly go to the wall'.*[170]

In August 1872 the South Midland Mining Engineers Institute made a visit to North Staffordshire to Heath's Biddulph Valley Ironworks, Ford Valley Ironworks and the Chatterley Company's Colliery at Whitfield as well as the Earl of Granville's deep pit at Hanley and ironworks at Etruria. Later in the day there was a lecture by a Dr Irvine of Glasgow on 'The Safety Lamp'. The day finished with a dinner and the customary toasts, one being proposed by Mr Rose to the Chairman and Vice Chairman.[171]

The Earl of Granville's Etruria Works as depicted in Griffiths' 'Guide to the Iron Trade.'

168. *The Shields Gazette*, 28th May 1869
169. *The Birmingham Daily Post*, 29th May 1869
170. *The Shields Daily Gazette*, 4th August 1869
171. *The Birmingham Daily Post*, 30th August 1872

Henry Fullwood Rose's application to the Institute of Mechanical Engineers

Topics at these meetings were many and varied. In May 1875, for instance, they discussed whether a miner should receive extra wages in lieu of their coal allowance.[172]

David was schooling his sons to follow him into the business. In December 1866 Henry Fullwood Rose was admitted as a member of the Institute of Mechanical Engineers. In 1869 William Napoleon Rose was admitted to the same institute. Both sons were nominated by George Addenbrooke. Henry's nomination was seconded by Joseph Foster Lloyd and William's by Henry John Marten, perhaps revealing the close working relationship of these families.

Henry Fullwood Rose was also a member of the Dudley & Midland Geological Society which made a visit to Hagley and Halesowen to look at the geological features of the Clent Hills. Like his father and uncle Thomas, Henry attended the meetings of the South Staffordshire and East Worcestershire Institute of Mining Engineers. Following another visit of the South Staffordshire Institute to their northern counterparts in August 1875, Henry was also elected a member of the North Staffordshire Mining Institute.

It was doubtless the discussions at such meetings which helped to guide the Rose family's decisions on investments.

172. *The Birmingham Daily Post*, 4th May 1875

9. Investments and speculation

As well as owning a number of ironworks and collieries, David Rose also invested both time and money in other concerns.

The Sandwell Park Colliery Company

In addition to his own mines David Rose was a shareholder in the Sandwell Park Colliery in the Walsall area. This colliery was developed by Henry Johnson in the early 1870s as the native Black Country coal supply began to be exhausted. The mine was over 1,200 feet deep and required a large investment.

The management of the colliery was problematic. A meeting of the shareholders was held in July 1877 to discuss the resignation of the directors of the company and to consider a new directorate and constitution of the Board. David Rose was in attendance. The existing directors appeared to have had a conflict of interest in that they had collieries of their own. A discussion took place on the level of investment needed to qualify as a director with the proposal that this should be fifty fully paid up shares. David Rose seconded the proposal, although it was not carried. The report indicated that there was considerable concern about the management of the colliery's affairs. The eventual outcome of the meeting was that a new board of directors was appointed. A suggestion was made that the colliery's engineer, Henry Johnson, be added to the board, although this was eventually rejected. David Rose proposed that a compensatory award of £100 be made to the directors.[173]

The concerns of the shareholders over the running of the colliery were soon to be justified. In November 1878 members of the North Staffordshire Mining and Mechanical Institute of Engineers made a visit to Sandwell Park. The group went underground to examine the workings. However, as one the cages was returning to the surface, *'Mr Arnold, of the firm Arnold and Garside, railway wagon builders, Stoke-on-Trent, and Mr Barker, engine builder, of Kidsgrove, tumbled backwards out of the cage and fell head foremost into the 'inset'. Mr Arnold sustained a bad fracture of the skull and other frightful injuries which at once rendered him insensible, and in about a quarter of an hour he expired in the pit ... Mr Barker also fell into the inset and rolled over into the cage hole which was about twelve to fourteen feet deep, with about eighteen inches of water on the top of a cage scaffold, which was placed in the 'sump'.'*[174]

Barker died shortly afterwards. Despite this and a series of other accidents, Sandwell developed into the first modern colliery in the Black Country, doubtless producing a return for David Rose and the other shareholders.

David also invested in the Nottingham Joint Stock Bank in September 1865 purchasing 20 shares at £50 each. The bank, opened by the lace manufacturer Thomas Adams, financed the rise of Jesse Boot's chemists. Other investments included 50 shares at £10 each in the Wolverhampton and Walsall Railway Company in May 1866 and 20 shares at £25 each in the Great Bridge Iron and Steel Company in October 1866.[175] However, he played a more active part in three other companies: The Globe Tube Works, The Staffordshire Financial Company and the Staffordshire Joint Stock Bank.

173. *The Birmingham Daily Gazette*, 27th July 1877
174. *The Tamworth Herald*, 9th November 1878
175. S.R.O.D1317 various.

The Globe Tube Works

The Globe Tube Works, in Wednesbury, was re-launched in July 1864 with David as one of the four directors, issuing 2,500 shares at £10 each. The works had originally been opened in 1849 by Cornelius Whitehouse who was responsible for turning Wednesbury into 'Tube Town'. There was a huge demand for tubes for steam engines and for gas lighting and Whitehouse invented a method to produce them cheaply and in greater lengths. The invention created a revolution in the trade and enabled his patron, James Russell, to increase his firm's production from 3,000 feet of tube in 1824 to over 5 million feet in 1865.

After Russell died, Whitehouse opened the Globe Tube Works but he was not a manager and, while other tube firms prospered, his struggled, hence the reconstitution of the business. The works were very extensive with premises covering over 7,500 square yards. The incentive

Cornelius Whitehouse, pictured in FW Hackwood, 'Wednesbury Faces, Places and Industries'

for David Rose and his fellow directors was that no remuneration would be given to the directors in any year unless the dividend was at the rate of at least ten per cent. At first the new firm's progress seemed encouraging with the directors issuing a report after six months declaring *'a dividend of 7 and a half percent for the period. This is the more gratifying to the directors, inasmuch as from the advanced season and other disadvantages under which they have had to labour, they did not anticipate as favourable a return, which moreover serves to increase their confidence in the soundness and future prosperity of the undertaking ...* '[176]

This soundness and prosperity did not last for long. The company continued into the 1870s, and even as late as 1873, adverts appeared encouraging investors to buy shares. Its demise was hastened by a fall in trade and an accompanying strike in late 1874 with workers protesting against a 10 per cent wage reduction.[177] In July 1878 the company was put into the hands of the liquidators who sought sums of £283 and £142 from David and Henry Rose respectively. David argued that he was a creditor of the company to the tune of £2,500 but the judge decided that both men still had to pay.[178]

The Staffordshire Financial Company

David Rose was also a substantial investor in the Staffordshire Financial Company, buying 100 shares at £10 each in September 1864.[179] Both David and William Napoleon Rose attended the second annual meeting with David, as a leading shareholder, proposing the re-election of two directors – Caleb Bloomer and Charles Britten. Caleb Bloomer was

176. *The Birmingham Daily Post*, 3rd February 1865
177. *The Birmingham Daily Post*, 2nd November 1874
178. *The Birmingham Daily Post*, 29th July 1878
179. S.R.O.D1317. op. cit.

also a director of the Whitehouse & Co Globe Tube Works.[180] Its accounts were published in the Birmingham Daily Post on an annual basis. We learn from a report of 1871 that its capital had dwindled in 1868 from £20,000 to £7,356 but it had then recovered to £11,823.181.[181] By 1876 this had increased to over £55,000.[182]

From a report in August 1879[183] we can see WH Duignan, David Rose's solicitor, was also one of the directors. A report in *The Birmingham Daily Post* in April 1865 shows that the first general meeting of the company was held in Duignan's offices. Duignan had a hand in many companies of this nature and it is quite likely that he introduced David to the possibilities of investing in them. A further example of the close connection between Duignan and David Rose in the investment world is seen in their involvement in the Staffordshire Joint Stock Bank.

The Staffordshire Joint Stock Bank

Shares in the Staffordshire Joint Stock Bank were far more expensive, costing £100 each. Both David Rose and William Duignan were both present in February 1866 at the second annual meeting of the Staffordshire Joint Stock Bank in Bilston, together with a number of other local industrialists such as Caleb Bloomer, Charles Rollason and Isaac Jenks.[184]

These companies proliferated after the passing of the Limited Liability Acts in 1855 and 1862. Checkland explains the principle behind such schemes. 'Down to the sixties business was mainly conducted either by the individual owner-manager, or by simpler partnerships ... But this system could be a serious limitation to the growth of business. It made for discontinuity, for the English partnership ended when any of its members died. By limiting the raising of capital to a relatively few men it could be most cumbersome. Finally, with each partner liable for the debts of the partnership to the full extent of his resources, the new extensions of business could be very risky. The solution was the creation of impersonal joint-stock corporations, in perpetuity, appealing to the public for capital, with a committee of directors in charge of policy, though responsible to the shareholders, and with the liability of each limited to the value of his subscribed shares.'[185]

The AGM of the Staffordshire Joint Stock Bank held in 1866 shows that it conformed exactly to this pattern. The Bank had branches in Wednesbury, West Bromwich and Walsall and had recently purchased the business of one of its shareholders, Mr Jones, to ensure the continuity of his company. Discussions centred on the healthy state of the Bank and its recent investments and a dividend of fifteen shillings per share was agreed.[186]

While the Staffordshire Joint Stock Bank appeared to be in good health, such institutions played a key part in the economic instability of the period. As Checkland also says, 'The very great increase in new projects called into being a frightening number of new companies under limited liability in the years 1863 and 1864. The new principle invaded most parts of

180. *The Birmingham Daily Post*, 1st August 1866
181. *The Birmingham Daily Post*, 1st August 1871
182. *The Birmingham Daily Post*, 1st August 1876
183. *The Walsall Advertiser*, 26th August 1879
184. *The Birmingham Daily Post*, 14th February 1866
185. SG Checkland, *'The Rise of Industrial Society in England'*, 1815-1885, p.107
186. *The Birmingham Daily Post*, 14th February 1866

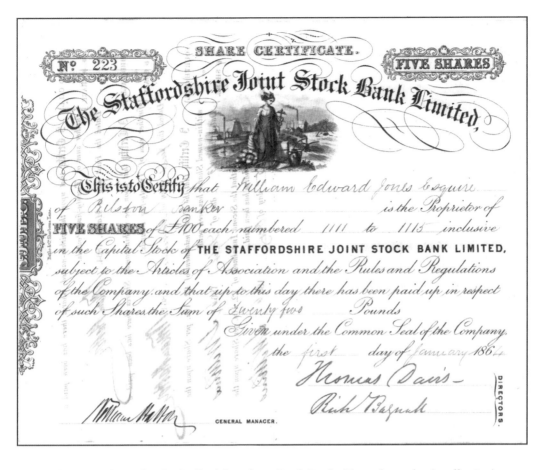

Share certificate for the Staffordshire Joint Stock Bank. (From the author's collection)

banking, commerce, transport and industry ... Business men were borrowing money for their permanent regular business, in order to use their own resources for joint-stock companies or foreign loans. Especially worrying were the new finance houses; would they, in their urge for profits and with their liabilities limited, abandon the conservative tenets of the sound old bankers ...The inevitable commercial crisis appeared in May 1866'.[187]

187. Checkland, op.cit. p43

10. Accidents in the Rose Ironworks

When David Rose began to establish his own iron and coal business in the 1850s scant attention was paid to matters of safety in either of those industries. Parliament had passed the Coal Mines Act 1842, which prohibited women and children from working underground and provided for the appointment of an Inspector of Mines. By 1853 there were just six inspectors for the entire country with its thousands of pits and by 1900 there were still only thirty inspectors. In the iron industry the picture was even bleaker. 'Minor accidents' were a common occurrence and not worth recording. The Children's Employment Commission of 1862 reported that: *'Owing to the quick and uncertain movements of the hot iron this employment is attended with much danger. Boys very rarely get through many turns without burns of a more or less serious character in their arms and legs ...'*[188]

It was not until 1864 that the law concerning safety guards on machinery was extended to cover factories other than those producing textiles. The *Birmingham Journal* recorded the death on 11th February 1854 of a ten year old boy, Charles Bagley, who worked at Thomas Rose's works in Bradley and who, *'becoming entangled in the machinery, was so much injured that he died the same afternoon.'*[189]

The Factory Act of 1867 significantly altered certain aspects of safety regulation contained in earlier Acts, for example transferring some responsibilities from factory occupiers to the owners of factory premises or owners of machines. A study of the accidents in the Rose ironworks reveals how factory and mine owners were gradually called to account. Indeed, it was an accident in an ironworks belonging to Thomas Rose, David's cousin, which led to attempts to improve boiler safety.

The first record we have of an accident in David's ironworks dates to1852 and occurred at the Victoria works in Leabrook, Wednesbury, shortly after he and Fletcher had gone into *partnership.* Two men were repairing a boiler when *'the steam valve from another boiler got loose and discharged the steam into the boiler where the two unfortunate men were. They were got out as soon as possible, but were both quite dead.'*[190]

David Rose's Old Hill Ironworks witnessed a fatality when repairs were being made to the furnace stacks. *'A man named James Slater, alias 'Cockin' (28), was at work at the 'lift' laying bricks, and had just remarked to one of his butty workmen that he had only got 18 inches laid, when he suddenly fell over the bricks, and was precipitated to the ground. When about 40 feet from the top the unfortunate man fell across an iron crane and then to the ground, inflicting a frightful gash in his head, and being killed on the spot. He leaves a wife and two children, and the wife is expecting another shortly.'*[191]

Other accidents were transport related. Daniel Rose was taken to court in March 1856 when one of his carriages with iron castings projecting over the side caused a collision and *'the plaintiff was thrown out of his cart, one of the shafts of which was smashed, and the horse ran away. The plaintiff, on the following Monday, called at the defendant's place of business and the clerk offered £2 as compensation. Mr Burton estimated the damage to the*

188. Children's Employment Commission, 1862, Third Report: Report on the Ironworks of South Staffordshire by FF Longe, p.xxvi
189. *The Staffordshire Advertiser*, 11th February 1854
190. *The Staffordshire Advertiser*, 24th April 1852
191. *The Birmingham Daily Gazette*, 28th October 1869

cart, horse and harness at £5, and the Judge, without hearing the evidence for the defence, gave the plaintiff a verdict for the whole amount of his claim. [192]

Three years later a fatal accident occurred when John Shaker, employed at Daniel Rose's Bull Bridge Works, was loading iron onto a cart: *'when the horse took fright and ran away. He attempted to stop the animal, but was knocked down by the shaft of the cart, and so severely injured that he had to be sent to his home, at Darlaston, where he died on the evening above named. The Jury returned a verdict of 'Accidental Death.'* [193]

The laying down of a railway track in 1872 from David Rose's Albert Works to the main line soon resulted in the death in September 1873 of hooker-on Edwin Prestidge. *'About midday on Saturday he was on one of the trucks when, by some cause or other, he slipped off, and fell below the rails and the trucks, several of which passed over the young man's body. When picked up – in two or three minutes afterwards – he was found to be dead, the injuries inflicted being of a shocking nature. Besides being otherwise mutilated, the body was nearly severed in two, and the right arm was nearly severed away by the wheels of the trucks. Deceased had only been engaged at this kind of work two days before the accident happened. The jury returned a verdict of 'Accidental death.'* [194]

The most shocking report of an accident in David's ironworks occurred in December 1870. William Carter, a fifteen year old boy was in charge of a boiler at the Moxley Works. The steam had escaped from the boiler and the boy had died in the South Staffordshire Hospital from the effects of the scalds he had sustained. Another worker, James Hazlehurst was slightly injured. [195]

The inquest considered two questions. The first being, who was responsible for the accident and the second being whether a boy of that age should have been put in charge of the boiler. The escape of steam was due to the water level in the boiler having sunk from two and a half feet to one foot. There was a water buoy attached which would have indicated the danger. All that was needed was to simply turn on a tap to add more water. It was established that the boy could have called for assistance to any number of men at any time should he have required it. The boiler itself had been recently inspected and was in good working order.

The Chief Engineer of the Midland Boiler Assurance and Inspection Company was called as a witness and testified that the law allowed boys of fifteen to supervise boilers. He also said that he did not recommend alarm whistles which were unreliable but suggested that a low water safety valve was the best means of preventing such accidents. However, these valves were very expensive and had not been adopted in South Staffordshire. The jury concluded that only the boy was to blame and recorded a verdict of accidental death.

Such accidents were very common. Two years earlier in September 1868, 11 people had been killed at Thomas Wells' Moxley factory. A boiler exploded and fortunately it was propelled across the canal side of the factory and not into the works, otherwise the casualty list would have been greater.

192. *The Staffordshire Advertiser*, 15th March 1856
193. *The Birmingham Daily Post*, September 1859
194. *The Birmingham Daily Post*, 12th September 1873; *Darlaston Weekly Times*, September 6th 1873
195. *The Birmingham Daily Post*, 10th December 1870

David Rose's scant regard for workers' safety is reflected in a case in 1879 when, *'Messrs Rose and Co. Moxley, were fined £1 and costs for having in their possession two illegal machines, £2 and costs under two several summonses for having certain unauthorised weights, and the costs of the proceedings were ordered to be paid touching ten 120lb. weights, which were also on the premises.'*[196] (The heaviest weight allowed was 56lb)

The Millfields disaster

Midlands Boiler Assurance and Inspection Company, mentioned above, had been set up after the horrendous explosion at David Rose's cousin, Thomas' factory in 1862. That safety was not Thomas' prime concern had been evident six years earlier, in 1856, when an accident occurred at his Bradley works where 70 to 80 people were employed. *'The centre one of three boilers exploded with a report that was heard for miles around, bringing down a chimney 60 feet high, tearing a neighbouring boiler from its bed, and ribbing up rolls and bedding. The roofing of the works and its surrounding brickwork were cast to an almost incredible distance. Massive iron uprights were broken to pieces, and scattered, with disjointed heavy machinery, upon every hand. The canal was nearly dammed up with the ruins which fell into it, sinking a longboat that lay near the works.'*[197]

Four men were killed and several injured. As a result, in July 1856 two men, William Tuckley, 21, and Henry Smith aged 19, were indicted for manslaughter, being charged with causing the deaths through not discharging their duty. They had been in charge of the boiler when it exploded and it was alleged that there was a deficiency of water. The whistle attached to the boiler which was there to warn of a water shortage, had been blocked up. The case revealed that there had been a leakage in the boiler six months previously which had been repaired. The defence argued that there were tin factories near Thomas Rose's works which deposited a large amount of sulphuric acid in the canal which fed the boiler. Both men were acquitted.[198]

The *Mining Journal*, commenting on the cause of such explosions, blamed the ignorance of the engineers but was more damning of the owners of such works who, *'possess so little spirit, or are so short-sighted in relation to their own interests, or so indifferent to the lives of others, as to neglect taking precautions.'*[199] The opinion of the Journal's correspondent was borne out in 1862 with the most devastating explosion to occur in any ironworks. Thomas Rose had gone bankrupt in the late 1850s but he was back in business in the early 1860s. The Millfields Works in Bilston had been in the possession of William Riley but the firm had accumulated £240,000 of debts in 1855. The works remained idle until they were purchased and reopened by Thomas Rose in February 1862.

Less than two months after Thomas Rose had begun production a catastrophic explosion occurred in April 1862 when twenty eight men lost their lives and many others were injured. A boiler exploded and a piece of it, weighing eight tons, was forced into the air to a height of over 200 feet and flew across the nearby railway line, demolishing three furnace chimneys. It landed in a field 300 yards away where it buried itself five feet in the ground.[200]

196. *The Staffordshire Sentinel*, 10th December 1879
197. *The York Herald*, 3rd May 1856
198. *The Staffordshire Sentinel*, 26th July 1856
199. *The Mining Journal*, 1856
200. *The Hereford Times*, 19th April 1862

A subscription was launched for the families of the deceased and was flooded with donations, including money from the workmen employed at David Rose's and Daniel Rose's Albert Ironworks, as well as from Henry Fullwood and William Napoleon Rose.[201]

A full report of the inquest was carried by the *Staffordshire Advertiser* over three weeks in April and May 1862.[202] There were many witnesses called to try and ascertain the cause of the explosion. Some of their testimonies were revealing. The boiler had been made in 1853 and had never had more than a quick inspection since it had been installed, and none since the works had been taken over by Thomas Rose. A month before, the night engineer, Richard Rowley, had noted a loose rivet, and ordered that a peck of bran should be poured into the boiler!

A Mr ET Wright, an engineer and ironmaster was requested by the coroner to make a thorough examination of the boiler. He found no evidence of a deficiency of water but discovered that the steam gauge was seriously defective in that it under-recorded the actual pressure. He concluded that the joint effects of oxidisation and old cracks had led to its giving way. He thought that boilers of that type were unsuitable for working non-condensing steam engines. Mr John Elwell, who made the boiler, testified that he found the stop box valve corroded and dirty and in his opinion had this not been the case the accident would not have occurred.

Abraham Leadbetter, who installed the boiler, said that he told Mr Riley, the previous owner, that it was too large for a high pressure engine, and he always considered it unsafe. Richard Jones, a shingler, said he had worked for Mr Riley, and while working had frequently run away in terror from the boiler. Richard Abbott, a pattern maker, who used to work for William Riley, said he considered that the boiler was a first-class one, but because it was so large and the fires that heated it so intense, it always required great vigilance on the part of the engineer to keep it from bursting. He had seen men run out of the works from fear of an explosion two or three times a week, and on one occasion he had been so terrified by fear that he could not move. Some were of the opinion that the boiler whistle had not worked for some time.

The coroner, in submitting the case to the jury, indicated that there was no evidence on which a charge of manslaughter could be preferred against the men in charge of the boiler when it burst. The jury returned a verdict to the effect that the boiler exploded from over-pressure of steam, but that there was insufficient evidence to show how this over-pressure was caused. They also expressed their opinion that boilers of the size and description of the one in question should not be used to work at high pressure. But no one was blamed for the explosion, least of all, Thomas Rose.

The explosion at Millfields was the trigger for the setting up of the Midlands Steam Boiler Inspection and Assurance Company in 1862. An experienced engineer and staff of inspectors were appointed to regularly inspect all the boilers insured by the Company, and give advice on their repair, alteration, and construction at a small annual charge. The owners of boilers were also to be able to insure their manufacturing premises against previously uncovered risks as well as to be able to 'alleviate the distress and destitution of the families

201. *The Birmingham Daily Post*, 17th May & 21st June 1862
202. *The Staffordshire Advertiser*, 19th April, 26th April & 3rd May 1862

of workmen' in the event of an accident.[203] By the end of 1862, 521 boilers were under inspection and 465 of these were insured. Despite all these efforts major boiler explosions continued.

The aftermath of the Millfields boiler explosion.   *(Courtesy Wolverhampton Archives Service)*

Unbelievably the following year, in October 1863, Thomas Rose's Bradley Bridge works were involved in another accident when a 40 horse power boiler exploded. Fortunately, the works had been stopped during the day for repairs to the puddling furnaces. Consequently there were few workmen on the premises, or the results must have been disastrous. In the event only one man was killed. Yet another inquest followed. The manager of the works said that two months previously the boiler had been examined by the engineer of the Midlands Boiler Inspection and Assurance Company, but that Thomas Rose had decided not to put the boiler in the scheme. This might indicate not only Thomas's penny pinching approach but also the cursory nature of the inspection.

As usual several witnesses were called to try and ascertain the reasons behind the explosion. In this case it seems to have been a case of human error. The reliability of engineer Joseph Hawthorn was questioned in the first hearing when witnesses reported that he had been seen unscrewing the stop valve of the boiler after the explosion had occurred.[204] While the inquest was adjourned another incident occurred which revealed the cavalier attitude of Hawthorn who was charged with gross misconduct and neglect. It was reported that: *'the alarm whistle attached to the boiler of which the prisoner, who was just concluding*

203. *The Birmingham Daily Post*, 17th May 1862
204. *The Birmingham Daily Post*, 29th October 1863

his night turn, was then in charge, was heard sounding very loudly, indicating a shortness of water. Several of the men, with the recent catastrophe fresh in their minds, and fearing another explosion, at once left off work, and betook themselves to a safe distance....The manager of the works at the same time went to the prisoner and ordered him to increase the supply of water. Under the belief that these directions had been attended to, the men resumed their work, but, as it afterward turned out, he had out of sheer idleness not only neglected to put in a supply of water, but had actually 'gagged' the steam-whistle to prevent it continuing the alarm, thus placing both his own life and the lives of his fellow workmen in imminent danger. He was committed to a month's imprisonment with hard labour.'[205]

So despite the efforts being made the explosions continued. Six people were killed at the Britannia Works at Bradley in December 1869. Another relief fund was launched to which David Rose contributed £5 but the *Birmingham Daily Gazette* was clear that something else had to be done. *'Unfortunately, boiler explosions, from their very frequency, attract but little attention beyond a mere passing chronicle in the general news of the day, and each one is almost forgotten as soon as the inquest is over ... We have before us a classified list of 1,046 boiler explosions by which 4,076 persons lost their lives, and 2,903 people were seriously injured ... A very general idea prevails that some strange and occult influences are continually at work in steam boilers. Hence has arisen a sort of indefinable feeling that a boiler explosion is usually an unavoidable calamity, like an earthquake, and that all concerned are not only objects of commiseration, but also free from blame. From its prevalence this idea has but too often found expression in the verdict of juries.'[206]*

The article identified three key causes of boiler explosions. Flaws were common in the original design and construction of boilers. The setting of the boiler usually made no allowance for contraction and this hampered inspection. In addition there were often defective fittings as well as ignorant or reckless working practices. It recommended that two internal safety valves be installed which could not be tampered with as well as water gauges. However, it was not until the Factories and Workshops Act of 1901 that the inspection of boilers was made compulsory.

In addition to accidents there were deaths often caused by the sheer hard work involved in ironworks. It was generally accepted that in some occupations, such as puddling, men were physically wrecked by the age of 45. One such case involved the death of a thirty-nine year old ball furnaceman, Samuel Martin, employed at David Rose's works in May 1864. Several witnesses were called including the underhand, Christopher Pointon who said that, *'when he got out his first heat, and was preparing for his second, he found him trembling violently. Witness placed him in a sitting posture. Some brandy was sent for, but before it arrived, the deceased, after two or three ineffectual efforts to vomit, almost instantly expired.'[207]*

The coroner seemed to want to attribute his death to Martin's alcohol intake but several witnesses said that his drinking was not excessive. Both Martin's wife and a fellow worker, William Humphries, testified that he was being treated for rheumatic fever. A verdict of death from natural causes was returned. Martin's widow was left with eight children to care for.

205. *Aris's Birmingham Gazette*, 21st November 1863
206. *The Birmingham Daily Gazette*, 16th December 1869
207. *The Birmingham Daily Post*, 12th May 1864

11. Health and safety and working conditions in the Rose collieries and brickworks

'The labouring population is, with exceptions…treated by their employers as mere brute instruments for the creation of wealth.' *Mines Inspector, Seymour Tremenheere*

The majority of the deaths that occurred in David Rose's operations were in his mines rather than in his ironworks. Some twenty men lost their lives in his collieries over a 30 year period. These were not unusual statistics with thousands of deaths occurring in the coal mining industry in the 19th century.

Miners at the Blue Fly Colliery, Wednesbury, c.1900. (Courtesy Sandwell Community History & Archive Service)

Even without accidents, conditions underground were grim. Gnats thrived in the heat. Rats and mice brought in accidentally with horse feed and hay bales, bred and multiplied. At the coal face men frequently worked naked to the waist. Life expectancy for miners in the 19th century was 10 years below the national average.

Colliers were hired for short periods, sometimes as day workers but more usually for one or two weeks at a time. A shift was defined as a 'stint', a flexible period of time defined by how long it took to dig a certain amount, commonly about 3 cubic metres of coal. 'Steady work' was not a feature of the industry. Earnings fluctuated depending on the price of coal. A foreman or 'doggy' was paid extra to enforce discipline underground. Insecurity of employment meant any dispute about safety or reluctance to follow orders was likely to result in dismissal. This approach was supported in the courts. In 1861, after entering into an agreement for 14 days' work but refusing to work in the pit, collier Thomas Garrington was sentenced by Wednesbury magistrates to 3 weeks' hard labour.

Yet wages were often higher than in other work and by the 1850s there were more than 25,000 miners in Staffordshire. However, the rate of accidental death in the Staffordshire coalfield far exceeded that experienced elsewhere in the country, averaging around 160 a year. The Black Country did not suffer the great pit disasters of Wales but deaths in ones and twos were regular. This pattern is followed by the accidents in David Rose's collieries.

Indeed, there was a period in the mid-1860s when fatalities in David Rose's mines contributed a fair percentage of the total in the area. Brough, the Inspector of the South

Staffordshire and Worcestershire district reported that between 1856 and August 1858, there were 20 fatal accidents, involving the loss of 63 lives in his area.[208] Nine of these deaths had occurred in David Rose's pits.

Roof falls

In mines everywhere falls of coal were responsible for more fatal accidents than any other circumstance. In the Black Country they resulted in more deaths than all other causes combined. They were so frequent that they were not usually reported to the coroner. There were two main contributory factors. Thomas Wynne, the first Mines Inspector for Staffordshire reported in 1852 that, *'There has been a melancholy loss of life from falls and I fear they will not decrease until a better system of management is introduced ... The only check on the avarice or caprice of the butty is the weekly visit of perhaps two hours duration from the ground bailiff or his assistant ... If the coal proprietors could be induced to take a deeper interest in their mining pursuits and in the welfare of the men whose lives are dependent on them a better system would soon be in operation.'*[209]

The second factor lay in the preferred method of mining in the Black Country. Coal was generally dug in thick seams using the pillar and stall method. Each miner worked individually to excavate a section of the face known as a stall or board. A thick pillar of undisturbed coal was left between stalls to act as a fire rib. Working from the bottom up, a thin upright column and a horizontal beam were left as supports. When the upper layers were undermined and the coal ready to fall, these were cut away and the upper strata brought down in a mass. It was an effective though wasteful way of working the Thick Coal and it was extremely dangerous. Pillars were vulnerable to collapse particularly under pressure in deep mines. Barnsby describes the procedure:

'The coal was undermined at the bottom and the various strata of coal 'piked' from above so that they fell to the floor of the pit ...The possibility of the undermined coal falling was always present. If this was avoided, the pikeman had to be extremely skilled to bring down his coals without burying himself. But the removal of the lower layers of coal was relatively simple compared with the problem of getting the upper layers. For this, the pikeman climbed on a plank suspended by chains from two ladders. In this situation the pikeman's life depended on his ears as he listened for the 'slip' which might bring down the coal before he removed the 'spurs' by which the coal was held before the pikeman was ready to bring it down. Beyond a certain height no tree tall enough to timber the roof could be brought into the pit ... a roof 30 feet high could not be timbered.'[210]

Many men favoured a method called longwall. By this method only half the height of the seam was worked in one operation and the other half removed in a second working but bailiffs objected to it because it involved more labour.

Fatalities in the Rose's pits were largely due to roof falls. Wooden props or sprags were often used but frequently were deficient in number.

208. *The Birmingham Daily Post*, 9th May 1859
209. Extract from Thomas Wynne's Mine Inspection Report, 1852, quoted by Barnsby, op. 210. cit.
210. Barnsby op.cit p.24

On 19th December 1855 James Lees was killed by a roof fall at Fletcher & Rose's Bradley Colliery.[212] In 1856 Joseph Green, aged 23, a pikeman, lost his life at Firehole No. 3 at the Bilston colliery due to a fall of shale.[213] On July 11th 1857, J Hitchen, a loader at Rose's Albert Colliery in Moxley, was killed by a: *fall of a stratum of coal ... One simple piece of timber would have prevented this accident.*[214] In October of the same year, 20 year old pikeman, J Shepherd, was killed when the roof, *fell upon him for want of spragging in disobedience of the 28th special rule.*[215] Spragging was the method of supporting the roof of a mine while undercutting the coal. Who had broken the rule is not said.

Year	Fatalities from roof falls in David, Daniel & Thomas Rose's pits	Fatalities Nationally[211]
1855	4	407
1856	1	400
1857	2	372
1858	6	376
1860	3	388
1868	1	444
1869	1	466

On 9th June 1858 W Wall, 15, a dirt carrier at Fletcher & Rose's Green Dragon Colliery, was killed by a fall of fireclay tops and bat, caused by a smooth faced slip.[216] On 11th December 1860 T. Hunt, aged 25, was killed at David Rose's Albert Colliery by a fall of coal. It was a new mine and was apparently 'well timbered'.[217]

211. Mining and Mineral Statistics of the United Kingdom of Great Britain and Ireland, 1884
212. The Coal Mining History Resource (CHRC)
213. CHRC
214. CHRC
215. CHRC
216. *The Walsall Free Press and General Advertiser* & CHRC
217. CHRC

We have more detail regarding a similar accident at the Waterloo Colliery in late December 1867 which resulted in the death of Joseph Fellows. *'The deceased and another man, named James Lynall, were engaged in taking up some sleepers and rails in a worked-out part of the colliery named, when he struck one of the rails against a tree, and that, falling down, brought down another tree and crossbeam, and dislodged a large quantity of dirt, which completely buried deceased and his companion, killing the former on the spot, and injuring the latter, but not seriously. No blame attaching to any person, the Jury returned a verdict of 'Accidental death'.*[218]

Fellows was a 'bandsman' or 'bondsman'. Such men were paid to shift the coal after it had been brought down by the pikemen. Skips were pulled along tramways to the bottom of the shaft where the load was attached by a hook to a flat rope called a band – hence the term bandsman or bondsman – following which it was hoisted above ground.

Daniel Rose's Moorcroft Colliery also witnessed fatalities from roof falls. There are a number of accidents recorded at the Moorcroft Colliery. One occurred in January 1857 resulting in the death of Thomas Simkin: *'The deceased was told by the doggy to put some sprags or supports under the coals he was cutting, and deceased said that he would go a bit further first. Whilst he was at work the coal fell upon the deceased, and injured him severely on the breast. Conveyed home and died the same day. Verdict, 'Accidental death.' E Brough, Esq, Government Inspector, attended.'* [219]

On March 5th 1860, another pikeman, Joseph Edwards, aged 30, was killed 'assisting to stand a tree in the No. 5 pit a mass of new mine coal came down. The colliery is very much pervaded by backs or slips.'[220] Slips were faults in the strata. On 30th September of the same year, Edward Jones, aged 30, another pikeman, was killed by a fall in a new mine at the Moorcroft Colliery. 'He actually sat down to smoke under these coals after they were holed and cut.'[221]

Similarly, Thomas Rose's pit at Rose Hill in Willenhall witnessed three fatal accidents due to falling coal in 1855. However, we have much greater detail on two other roof fall accidents at David Rose's collieries, both of which illustrate the struggle to apportion blame and responsibility. The first of these occurred in April 1858 when a boy and three men by the names of Lamb, Kelly, Hudson and Cuniffe, aged 16, 22, 23 and 53 respectively were crushed by a fall of 15 tons of coal at David Rose's Green Dragon Pit, part of the Bradley Colliery.

At the first inquest, Edward Hosling described the scene. *'The first sight that presented itself was that of a boy named Joseph Lamb, about 18 years old, who suddenly became partially buried under a heavy fall of coal. He was, however, soon extricated, but not without sustaining severe injuries. It was then made known that three men were under the heaviest fall of coal, and it was not until after great efforts on the part of the doggy and the other workmen that the three bodies were discovered, which fully occupied the men upwards of an hour.*

218. *The Birmingham Daily Post*, 4th January 1868
219. *The Birmingham Journal*, 10th January, 1857
220. CHRC
221. CHRC

'The deceased Cunniff was found in a sitting posture inside his basket, but seemed to have been struck upon the breast and temples and forced backwards. The deceased Kelly had been struck upon his head and shoulders, for when his body was discovered the head and feet were nearly together, with his face to the floor of the pit.'

The inquest then began to focus on why the accident had occurred with the Mines Inspector, Mr Brough reporting that there was a dearth of timber supports: 'There was only one tree set up, and that a very ineffectual one in strength, whereas the stall demanded at least six trees instead of one for the protection of the loaders – that was to say, three trees ought to have been stuck up on each side of the railroad, and this the men would have been saved. These trees were more than usually required on account of the great number of smooth-faced slips that were evident to anybody looking up to the bottom of the 'four foots.' Mr Brough added that if the proper timber had been set up in the manner he had described the men would certainly not have been killed.'

The mine agent, Cope and two other miners, Joseph Lunn and John Branaghan all testified that they thought the roof was sufficiently supported. The Coroner advised the jury to return a verdict of accidental death.[222]

It is in this light that we have to consider why 'D. Rose' was so involved in the election of the local coroner in 1860.[223] We do not know if this was David or his brother Daniel, but both of them may have had a vested interest in the outcome. The successful candidate was a Mr Jackson whose campaign involved meetings in various local districts held with 'freeholders and gentlemen' and setting up committees of supporters. One of the Wednesbury Committee's members was a D Rose. It was entirely possible that the successful appointee would take a more lenient line on accidents in the works of his supporters.

One way of focussing the owners' attention was by prosecution. However, it was often those they employed who faced charges. This was the case with the four fatalities in the accident at the Green Dragon Pit. A month after the accident a summons was taken out by Inspector Brough against Vernon Danks and Thomas Webb who were charter masters at the Green Dragon. David Rose provided his own solicitor, Mr Duignan, to make the case for the defendants. The case rested on the interpretation of the Coal Mines Act. The prosecution alleged that the defendants were liable according to: 'the 20th section, which went to show that the charter master or his deputy should, where no other person was appointed for that purpose, examine the shaft, side-wheels, inset and sump, at least once a day, and should give notice, when such repairs were necessary as to require it, to the manager or his deputy, whose duty it should be to see them done.'

Duignan contended that the defendants, under the 28th rule, were not liable 'inasmuch as every collier was to securely sprag or spurn the coal whilst holing, and also prop when necessary the roof of the place in which he was working, and if he should not be provided with props he was to cease working, and report the same to the manager'.

Many of the witnesses called were the same people who testified at the inquest. Brough again bore witness to the lack of timbering. Duignan argued that in the two inquests the juries had returned a verdict of accidental death. The magistrate, Mr Leigh, observed,

222. *The Birmingham Daily Post*, 6th April 1858; The Staffordshire Advertiser, 17th April 1858
223. *The Birmingham Daily Post*, 23rd August 1860

however, that there must be a conviction and that the witnesses for the defence were interested parties whose evidence carried little weight. The defendants were therefore fined 40 shillings each plus costs.[224] The fine was a pittance but it was the maximum that had been set by the 1855 Coal Mines Inspection Act when men were prosecuted. Brough had previously expressed disappointment that the rules were not more stringent.

The rate of prosecution was still very low. As Barnsby notes, the procedure was difficult and time consuming. Evidence had to be collected, the Coroner's findings taken into account and the Secretary of State's permission to initiate a prosecution obtained. In 1863, W Bennett of Coseley, writing to the *British Miner*, condemned the composition of juries in mining cases. He questioned what they knew of mines and claimed they brought in verdicts of accidental death where it should have been manslaughter or murder. When owners were prosecuted they tended to be small men. There is no evidence of the owners of the largest pits, the Earls of Dudley, ever being prosecuted. The percentage of miners killed in his pits varied from 10% in the 1850s to 20% in the 1860s.

Ultimate accountability remained uncertain until a legal precedent set in 1867 made clear that this was not something owners could delegate. David Rose was soon to find this out. That the law was beginning to be tightened and enforced was in evidence concerning a case at David Rose's Old Hill Colliery. In March 1869, Joseph Male, the doggy, was brought to court by David Rose's mine agent, Henry Johnson: *'for a breach of the colliery rules. Before any one is permitted to go down the doggy is bound to examine the pit. According to the special rules, he ought to have fetched the men back or followed them down immediately. Complainant did not wish the bench to inflict heavy punishment upon the defendant, but would be satisfied if he were reprimanded.'* The Chairman made the point that Male was extremely fortunate since had a fatality occurred he would have faced a charge of manslaughter.[225]

Yet, the very next day a fatality did occur when John Hickman was crushed by a fall of coal at the same pit. Again an inquest was held and a verdict of accidental death was once again returned. However, two months later, the Mines Inspector brought a case against David who was charged with having neglected to publish certain special rules at the Old Hill Colliery. The 1855 Coal Mines Inspection Act had specified general rules applicable to all collieries and a set of special rules for each colliery district. The rules that had been drawn up at Old Hill did not conform to a colliery which was managed by the owner or his agent. It was not until the fatal accident occurred that the Mines Inspector was aware of the discrepancy. Despite the arguments of Duignan, Rose's solicitor, the chair of the magistrates *'enlarged on the serious nature of the case, inasmuch as the amendment to the rules not being adopted, there was no one responsible if anything went wrong at the colliery ... The very lowest fine they could impose was £5 and costs ... Mr Duignan said it was the first time that Mr. Rose had been fined under the Act.'*[226]

Punishments were later stepped up under pressure from miners' associations. The 1872 Coal Mines Regulation Act made it compulsory to employ a competent manager at every colliery with a workforce of more than thirty. Managers and owners faced imprisonment

224. *The Birmingham Daily Post*, 6th May 1858
225. *The Birmingham Daily Gazette*, 25th March, 1869
226. *The Birmingham Daily Post*, 26th May & 16th June 1869

for wilful neglect and breaches of the law. However, many of the collieries in the Black Country employed fewer than thirty men and the accidents continued.

Gas

Besides roof falls, the dangers of gas were ever present. The earliest record of a fatal accident caused by gas in the Rose collieries comes in 1853 when three men were killed in an explosion at Thomas Rose's colliery in Willenhall.

Three fatalities occurred due to gas in David Rose's collieries. John Butler died at Rose's colliery at Bilston on the 30th April 1857. Butler, aged 36, was a Deputy. It was reported that, *'The air had been cut off to turn it into another channel and as all beyond the point remained for a short time unventilated, orders were issued that no one should approach the place at all until a door was put up; but this man went to get a rail leaving his candle stuck on the rib and of course, when he returned, he brought just enough gas out to fire at the candle and explode all that part of the pit.'*[227]

The second incident occurred in David Rose's Albert Colliery in 1873 when George Foster, a butty, and Joseph Blakemore, the doggy, both died having thought they had cleared the danger of gas. One version of events was that *'on reaching the bottom they called out 'All right', and told William Foster to descend, and that when he did so he found them dead or dying. There seems no doubt that they were overcome by the after-damp or choke-damp. Both were men of experience, and are spoken of as of careful habits in their work, although their descent as soon after the fire-damp would seem to show a great want of caution in this instance.'*[228]

Clause 32 of the Coal Mine Regulation Act of 1872, which had been passed the year before this accident, stated that the chartermaster or overman should, if any part of the mine is in a dangerous state, *'withdraw the workmen from the mine, or such part thereof, and the competent person appointed for the purpose shall immediately inspect the same, if the danger arises from inflammable gas, with a locked safety lamp and shall make a true report of such examination in the book kept for the purpose, and shall sign the same, and shall forbid any workman to re-enter the mine or such part thereof as was found to be dangerous, except for the purpose of examination or repair, until the same is stated by a further report not to be dangerous.'*

In addition, Clause 49 stated that *'No Collier shall under any pretence light any blower or accumulation of gas ... or do any act whereby the ventilation of the mine may be affected, or the safety of the workmen, or the property of the owner endangered.'*

However, many butties often engaged in cost-cutting. Whether any corners had been cut in this case was investigated in a prosecution in January 1874 when the mine manager, Thomas Brettle was charged with neglecting to provide proper ventilation. Brettle pleaded guilty but argued that: *'he had provided for them a plentiful supply of air which the men, however, without the defendant's knowledge had failed to use, because they considered they should have retarded progress. Further, the defendant had appointed a qualified deputy, and was absent at the time of the fatal occurrence.'*[229]

227. CHRC
228. *The Morning Post*, 28th August 1873
229. *The Birmingham Daily Post*, 23rd January 1834

What emerges from the case is the belief that the measures of the Coal Mines Regulation Act of 1872 were particularly stringent. The Stipendiary Magistrate summed up by saying that the Act was stern and that Brettle had taken reasonable measures but it was evident that, not only should the colliery rules be published, but that they should be verbally communicated to the men. A fine of £5 was imposed – again this was the maximum that could be levied on an owner. At least some progress had been made in ascertaining that miners should actually be spoken to about the rules.

Some improvements had been made in ventilating mines but the Black Country continued to rely on natural ventilation. Opposition to the Act came from the belief that any further improvement would encourage the spontaneous combustion to which the large amount of slack in the coal workings was liable. In addition, Davy's safety lamp was not adopted in this district, the colliers preferring to work with candles because the lamp gave a poor light and reduced the amount of coal they could send to the pithead. In 1873 there were only 44 such fatal accidents recorded nationally.

Falling down the shaft

A third cause of fatalities in the collieries was men falling down the pit shaft. This type of accident is also in evidence in David Rose's collieries. 12 year old C Tranter died in December 1864 when he fell into the sump of the pit shaft at the Moxley Colliery.[230] Fatal accidents of a similar nature, recorded nationally in 1864, totalled 158.

More detail is given on Isaac Wilkinson aged 66 who fell sixty feet to his death in November 1867 in one of David Rose's pits in Moxley. He *'went to the top of the shaft, and moved as if he was stepping into the bowk. Whether or not the bowk was attached to the chain, or whether the deceased, in putting his foot into it, forced it on one side against the brickwork and unhooked it, those present at the time could not tell; but the deceased disappeared, and as was seen ascertained, fell to the bottom of the shaft ... There being no direct evidence to show how the deceased fell down the shaft, the Jury returned an open verdict. Mr Harvey, the manager of the colliery, by the suggestion of the Coroner, undertook to have a collar placed so as to keep the handle of the bowk fast on the hook at the end of the gin chain.'*[231]

The Coal Mines Regulation Act of 1872 which came in 5 years later would have prevented such an accident, stating that: *'The Banksman shall in all cases give the proper signal, according to the code, Rule No. 59, to the Engine Tender to lower the skip or cage, and shall never allow any person to go down the pit when at work, until he has given the proper signal to the Engine Tender and Hooker-on, or Cager, and received the returned signal.'*

A similar accident occurred at Thomas Rose's pit in Buckley. James Hall, a sinker at the colliery, died on February 1st 1866, *'falling out of the tub in the sinking pit.'*[232]

We are reminded of how, on a daily basis, a miner was always close to death by a description of a near accident in September 1874: *'On Thursday morning last two sinkers, named Thomas Maddocks and John Norton, engaged in sinking a shaft (No. 4 Albert Colliery) belonging to Mr David Rose, Moxley, which is now about 130 yards deep, had*

230. CHRC
231. *The Birmingham Daily Post*, 3rd December 1867
232. CHRC

fired a shot, and were being drawn up to the top, when, about 30 yards from the surface, the crank of the engine broke. The engine tender, William Bradley, instantly put on the brake. The men remained suspended in the shaft a little more than one hour; whilst the chief engineer, Mr Samuel Whitmore, was brought to the spot, and, with assistance, both men were raised to the surface. Too much praise cannot be given to Bradley for his promptitude in applying the brake. [233]

A bowk being emptied at Sandwell Park (Jubilee) Colliery c.1890.

(Courtesy Sandwell Community History & Archive Service)

Other accidents

Some accidents were caused by a combination of freak weather and lack of maintenance. One such accident occurred in November 1865 at David Rose's Broadwater Colliery when a severe gale hit the area and part of the chimney stack blew down, leading to the death of sixty year old Isaac Fellows, an engine tender. Fortunately the engineer, John Evans halted the winding engine to avert a further accident at the pit mouth. Again no blame was apportioned at the inquest.

'It was shown that the stack was built about twenty-eight years ago, and although it was out of the perpendicular, and was seen to rock on the morning in question, no danger was apprehended. It was secured by two iron rods passing inside the stack from the base to the summit, a distance of some fifty feet, but these were snapped asunder when the erection gave way. There was no reason to suppose that any person had been guilty of negligence, and therefore, deeming no further evidence necessary, the Jury returned a verdict of 'Accidental Death'. [234]

In 1875, there was another stark reminder of the cost of extracting coal. *'On Wednesday a fatal accident occurred at No 1 A Pit belonging to David Rose and Sons, by which a miner, named Thomas Allen, living at Dangerfield Lane, lost his life. It appears the deceased was in the act of blasting a rock, when the charge went off, breaking both his legs, and driving a piece of rock clean through his stomach. Death was instantaneous. An inquest will be held.'* [235]

233. *The Birmingham Daily Post*, 12th September 1874
234. *The Birmingham Daily Post*, 27th November 1875
235. *The Wednesbury, West Bromwich and Darlaston Examiner*, 16th January 1875

It was not until much later that new rules governing shot-firing were introduced as electrically detonated compounds began replacing gunpowder and fuse. Some accidents occurred through sheer tiredness. On November 16th 1884 the watchman at Rose's Broadwaters Colliery, John Davis, aged 57, fell from a boiler seat in the dark. He died 6 days later.[236]

The only financial recompense for families affected by accidents in the mines was the fact that owners, butties and miners often collectively contributed to sick pay and widows' allowances. Miners usually paid an agreed levy whenever there was a serious incident. As the 19th century progressed, miners took out life and accident insurance.

As some of the collieries began to fall into disuse in the 1880s they still remained death traps. One day in July 1885 thirteen year old Caroline Rotchell, who had just taken her father's supper to him at David Rose's ironworks, stopped to play with other children at the Old Gin Pit in Colliery Field, part of David Rose's Woods Bank Colliery. She *'was swinging on a 'gin' along with other children ... got inside the 'drum' the centre part of the winding apparatus, and whilst the other children were pushing the gin' round she put her head through an aperture at the top of the 'drum' the result being that her neck was broken. The Jury returned a verdict of 'Accidental death'. The Coroner suggested that the apparatus should be firmly secured. Mr Davies, who represented Messrs Rose, promised that this suggestion should be carried out, and also pointed out that the proprietors of the colliery had frequently attended to it.* '[237]

The colliery informed the coroner that the apparatus was usually secured but the children always managed to bypass any security measures that they put in place.

Conditions in David Rose's brickworks

The area around Moxley had plenty of clay for brickmaking. Bricks were used extensively in blast furnace construction and often had to be replaced. David Rose set up his own brickworks and these feature in the report by the Children's Employment Commission of 1871 written by Francis Longe. It was estimated that there were between twenty and thirty thousand children between the ages of 5 and 16 employed nationally in brickyards. Longe began by describing the conditions which generally prevailed in such works.[238]

'The system of employment in the large brickyards is as follows: the employer uses machinery for preparing the clay, and employs girls of 16 years and upwards, in many cases married women, to mould the bricks. The moulders are paid about 2s 10d. or 3s per 1,000 and make from 1,500 to 2,000 bricks a day. Each moulder employs two or three girls or little boys to fetch the clay from the clay hole or pit and carry off and lay the moist bricks when moulded. The girls, if only two, are generally about 12 to 17 years of age. When the moulder employs three girls, which is generally the case, the third child is about 8 or 9 years old ... Many girls told me they had begun about 6 or 7 years of age. When I mention that I found in one yard little girls of 4 years old, who had been coming to work regularly for some weeks to help another sister of about 7 years of age in carrying clay for their elder sister of 17, the character of the system can be easily appreciated. Of course the child of 4

236. CHRC
237. *The Tamworth Herald*, 11th July 1885
238. Children's Employment Commission, 1871, The Brickyards of South and North Staffordshire

years old was only supposed to be beginning, but when at work she was taking her part in the manufacture as much as her elder sister ...

'*The severity of the labour undergone depends much upon the distance over which the clay and bricks have to be carried. Generally the clay hole is only a few yards from the tables, and about four feet below the level of the stove. The moist clay is projected into this pit by the pug mill. The girls thrust their arms into the heap of clay, and grab together as much as they are able to carry out at a time. They carry one lump on the head and another in their arms. In many of the smaller yards, the bricks are made near the pits from which the clay is dug. The clay is tempered by men at the bottom of the pit, and carried up to the tables by the girls.'*

Longe supported his report with references to specific brickyards, including that owned by David Rose. '*In one such yard at Moxley I found a girl of 24 making 2,000 bricks a day, and having two girls, one of 15 and the other of sixteen years of age, to carry clay and lay her bricks. These girls had to carry the 10 tons of clay, which she used in the day, up the slippery sides of the pit from a depth of about 10 yards, and over a distance of about 70 yards.*'

One of the testimonies given to the Commission was by Anne Wooley who worked at David Rose's Moxley brickworks. Her father, sister and their lodger were all employed in brickmaking.[239] '*I began when I was 15. I mould now. I am 24. I am paid by the thousand.*

Children carrying loads of clay in one of the brickyards of the English Midlands. Illustration from The Graphic *(London, 27th, May 1871)*

239. 1861 Census for Darlaston

I have 2 girls to carry clay. One is going 16 and the other 15. I make about 2,000 bricks in a day. I have to work the whole time from 6 to 6 to do that. I always stop half an hour for breakfast and 1 hour for dinner. (N.B. The clay carriers at this yard had to carry the clay from the bottom of the pit to the table at the top; the ascent was about 10 yards in 70 yards.)'

Perhaps the incident which casts the longest shadow on the attitude of the Roses was one which occurred outside their works. We do not know whether the reference is to David or his brother Daniel but it occurred in January 1847 when the brothers were jointly running the Moxley Ironworks. A 67 year old man Charles Russell was injured by a cart on the Moxley road. His leg was broken and an artery ruptured. He was taken to one of the nearest premises but a Mr Rose refused to take him in or even assist taking the injured man to the nearby works of Mr Wells. The man subsequently died.[240]

The Rose's treatment of their own workers was often particularly self-centred as we will examine in the next chapter.

240. *The Staffordshire Advertiser*, 27th January 1847

12. Charitable giving and the treatment of workers

As with many industrialists in the Victorian period, there were two sides to David Rose. One was his public face of charitable donations following the paternalistic pattern of men of his position. The other was his treatment of his own workforce - leaving aside areas such as health and safety and working conditions.

David gave donations to several funds and institutions. The earliest record we have of David Rose's charitable giving is in December 1854 with donations made to the Patriotic Fund in aid of Crimean War widows. David Rose donated £10, his wife £2 2s and Henry Rose £2 2s.[241] There is also a list of donations made in February 1855 by Fletcher & Rose's workmen at the Albert Ironworks, as well as a list of donations from miners at Bradley Colliery.

Fletcher & Rose made donations to the Birmingham and Midland Eye Institution and David continued to do this on a regular basis even when he was struggling in the late 1850s. In 1874 he doubled his subscription from one to two guineas.[242] The South Staffordshire Hospital was another beneficiary with David Rose making a hefty donation of £27 19s in early 1870.[243] The previous year the men at the Albert Works contributed over £29 while those at the Moxley Ironworks gave over £6. The Moxley Ironworks made a further donation of £12 6s 3d in 1871 which was apparently their second contribution that year.[244]

A prize medallion struck for the Dudley & Midland Exhibition   (Author's collection)

Donations were also made to the Wolverhampton Orphan Asylum. This may have been an institution that was close to his heart bearing in mind that David had lost his father at an early age. Gifts were made both in cash and in kind. In 1864 David gave £52 10s while in 1868 his wife donated £21. In 1866 a delivery of coal was made to the Asylum.[245]

David Rose's family were also patrons of education. In February 1862 Henry Fullwood Rose gave a lecture on Oliver Goldsmith in aid of funds for the Moxley Reading Room.[246] Then, in early 1867, a performance of Handel's Messiah was given at St James' New School Room in Wednesbury. Tickets were five shillings and the proceeds went towards paying for the cost of the

241. *The Staffordshire Advertiser*, 23rd December 1854
242. *The Birmingham Gazette*, 11th May 1857; *The Birmingham Daily Post*, 16th December 1874
243. *The Birmingham Daily Post*, 2nd February 1870
244. *The Staffordshire Advertiser*, 16th January 1869; *The Birmingham Daily Post*, 6th September 1871
245. *The Staffordshire Advertiser*, 25th June 1864, 6th January 1866 & 5th December 1868
246. *The Birmingham Daily Post*, 26th February 1862

Opening of the Wolverhampton exhibition 1869.   (Courtesy of Wolverhampton Archives Service)

building. Both David and his son, Henry were listed as members of the Oratorio Committee which organised the event.[247]

David Rose and the Dudley and Midland Exhibition

David Rose was also keen to educate his own workforce. An exhibition on local industry and fine arts was opened in July 1866 in Dudley. This was one of several that were organised in the area and although we have no visual record of the Dudley Exhibition there is a photograph of one that was held in Wolverhampton in 1869. The Dudley Exhibition attracted many visitors including, in late September, men from David Rose's works. The manner of their visit made quite an impact.

> *'On Saturday last the Exhibition at Dudley was visited by about 450 persons, in the employ of Mr. David Rose, of the Albert Iron Works, Moxley. At a very early hour in the morning of the day flags were flying from the tops of the stacks and other prominent parts of the works, and a very handsome decoration of evergreens and colours was erected over the principal entrance.*

247. *The Birmingham Daily Gazette*, 31st December 1866

At twelve o'clock the men formed a procession, headed by the band of the Wednesbury Rifle Corps, Mr Rose and members of the family in their private carriage, and the clerks and managers. Their route lay through Moxley and Bilston to Coseley Street Station, and the extent of the procession, the flags, banners, and other decorations, together with the excellent music performed by the band, formed an imposing spectacle for the inhabitants of the streets through which they passed on their way to the railway. They were conveyed to Dudley by a special train, and walked again in procession to the Exhibition, the varied and interesting objects of which engaged their attention for three hours.

Upon their return to the works at Moxley at six o'clock, they were entertained by Mr Rose at a sumptuous dinner of roast beef, plum pudding, and ale, in a large building which had been cleared out, fitted up and lighted with gas for the occasion.' [248]

David Rose's Truck Shop: fair treatment of the workers?

We get a very different picture of David Rose when we look at how he operated his shop. Like many of his fellow industrialists, David Rose set up his own shop at Moxley which was investigated by the Truck Shop Commission of 1871. The Truck System compelled workers to spend a proportion of their wages in the factory shop. In many communities ironmasters were able to dominate the local economy by the use of this system. The system had been declared illegal in 1831 but there were many loopholes. The penalties for violation of the Act were inadequate, being a fine of £10 for a first offence, £20 for a second and £100 for a third violation. In addition, prosecution was only possible if an individual brought the accused before two local magistrates who had the power to impose fines.

The Moxley shop featured in a court case reported in December 1870 when, *'Messrs Henry and William Rose, provision dealers, Moxley, were charged with having had a pair of meat scales half an ounce against the purchaser. Mr Salter appeared for the defence. It was shown that the defect was due to the scales having been temporarily placed upon an uneven surface, instead of in their usual position. The case was dismissed.'* [249] Why they had been moved in the first place was not mentioned!

There are two key sources for examining how David Rose's shop actually worked. One is the report of the Truck Shop Commissioners[250] and the other is a series of letters which appeared in the local press at the time. The letters give a different perspective on the shop compared to the evidence given before the Commission. The Truck Commissioners Report reveals that the shop was a large concern serving some 458 workers employed by David Rose in Moxley.

The men were obliged to spend some of their pay there. It had been opened in April 1870 by David's sons, William and Henry, by which time the men were being paid fortnightly. If they needed money in the meantime they had to go to the office and ask for a 'draw' or advance. There were reported cases of men losing their jobs if they didn't draw

248. *The Wolverhampton Chronicle and Staffordshire Advertiser,* 26th September 1866
249. *The Birmingham Daily Post,* 14th December 1870
250. Report of the Truck Commission, Part 11 – Special Reports, 1871

from the shop. The amount drawn in the first six months of 1870 was £5,625 and that £410 6s 9d was spent in the shop in a three month period.

James Henry Cottam was manager of the shop and was assisted by a butcher and a counter man. Cottam's testimony reveals that he had run a similar shop for David Rose some thirteen years before, when the men were paid in checks (tokens) instead of money. Jacob Bell, listed as a cashier at Rose's works, also gave evidence at the inquiry. The line of questioning when he was interviewed established the procedure at the Moxley works.

'Where is the draw given to the men? – At the office.
At the same office at which the wages are paid? – Yes.
Is that at the weighing machine? – Yes
Within the works? – Yes.
And close to the shop? It is not far from it.....About 200 or 300 yards, perhaps.
Then, when the men get their draw at the weighing machine, are they expected to take a portion of it to the shop? – They are expected to take a portion of it as a rule.
And do they go from the place where they receive the draw to the shop? – Sometimes.
Do they as a rule? Yes.'

Bell also said that on occasion if someone had not spent their draws at the shop then they would be refused draws the next time. The examiner then produced a paper from the works which had 3 columns - one representing the amount of draw, the second, the person or family who came for it and the third, the amount that had been spent at the shop. This was checked the next time a man came in the office for a 'draw.' Cottam said that barely a quarter of the men used the shop but said he didn't know how many were employed! The Commissioners also heard evidence from some other employees, as well as William Rose himself who testified that it was expected the men would shop there, but reported that the profits had not been satisfactory. He was challenged on this by the examiner who remarked that the first few months of any shop were the most difficult. The enquiry noted that Mr Rose had called some of his men to give evidence and that the influence brought to bear on them was freely admitted.

At the same time as the Commissioners were hearing evidence, a number of letters appeared in the *Birmingham Gazette* as part of a series of reports on the Truck System. These give further insight into David Rose's shop. The most revealing was published in early November 1870. Workers may not have been willing to take their case to the magistrates but they were not shy of making their views known through the newspapers. Even when taking into account possible bias on the part of the letter writer, the report reveals the very tight hold that the Rose's had on their workers' spending as well as the considerable amount of dissatisfaction among members of the workforce.

The letter reveals that there were now eight pawnshops in Darlaston as a result of the increasing hold of Tommy Shops, although the employers of course did not describe them as such. The writer pointedly remarked that: *'A rose by any other name would smell as sweet;'* and the *'Albert Stores'* – a euphemism sufficiently suggestive of something great and good - have, since February last, rendered any *'Tommy Shop'* in Moxley quite unnecessary.' At no point in the report does the writer refer to the Roses by name but it is clear that they are the owners in question. One wonders if the phrase 'a rose by any other name' was deliberately chosen. The report then goes into more detail on how the writer had gathered his evidence. *'Last Friday was draw day at the great Moxley establishment. I* chanced to be in close proximity to the works at the time, and saw a good many women, apparently the wives of workmen, trudging home with their bundles, which consisted of flour, grocery, meat and other articles - goods which in any other part of the Black Country, would have been designated by the generic name of 'Tommy'. They were not at all afraid of telling me what class of goods were sold at the 'store', and even freely communicated the measure of fancy prices exacted for some of them.

Flour, for instance, cannot be purchased at the 'Albert Stores' except at a positive advance of threepence per stone on what are called market prices; meat is, on the whole, relatively cheaper, but breasts of mutton – certainly not the most tempting of joints at any time – are charged 9d per lb. Tea, sugar, and in fact, everything of that kind, is at least 15 per cent dearer than at the ordinary tradesmen's shops. The articles dealt in here are almost as those found in a Yankee dry goods store: from clothing, hats and caps, drapery and haberdashery, boots and shoes, down to oyster-knives, pudding tins, carpet slippers, and clothes-pegs.'

The writer then proceeded to relate the stories told to him by one of David Rose's employees. *'A workman told me that, wanting a pair of boots a week or two since, he inquired the price at the 'store' and found this to be about 3s more than he could purchase them for in Bilston. ... While trade is good,' he continued, 'the men are not much complained on for not going to the shop, but if there comes a slack time they'd be sure to be picked out and discharged. Trade's very good here now with the puddlers, and they're setting more men on almost every day.* (The Albert Works was expanding with the building of the blast furnaces). *Not perhaps, so good as some, for they're getting 'em at as low wages as they con. These sort, you know, sir, bain't able to put anythin' by for a time o' sickness or what not, and if – as like as not – any accident happens and kills one on 'em, the hat has to be sent round to raise the money to bury him ...*

My informant was evidently in a communicative mood, for he went on to say that every man about the place 'wished to God the shop would close' ... The several foremen here kept small shops, which were managed by their wives and families, prior to the inauguration of the 'Albert Stores', but it was significantly hinted to them that the shops must be discontinued or they must leave their employment. They continue at work, and the little shops are closed ...

Another of the workmen, in a lower grade, who has to go to the 'Tommy Shop', says: 'My wages are not worth more than 17s a week to me now we have to go to the shop, although I earn £1.' The wife of a foreman at Moxley informed me that she had not been to the 'store' for three weeks, and while in the mind she was then, 'she didn't mean to go again'. Her chief grounds of complaint were of the inferior articles and very high prices. Fully aware of the penalty attached to such obstinacy, she vowed she didn't care. 'It will take them all their time to find another man to do my husband's work,' she said, 'and they can't well do without him.

One of the men working at Moxley told me his story. He had worked there a few months, and had been a tolerably steady patron of the 'store'. To the shopman he one day said, 'I've always spent my money at the shop; I want it next week for something else – how will it be if I take it away?' 'Well,' was the reply, 'you'll get no draw again when you want it.'

While some expressed their frustration by boycotting the Rose's shop, others reacted to their situation in a more direct fashion.

71

13. Industrial relations in the iron and coal industries and the impact on the Rose works

Tensions in the iron industry

Relations between workers and employers in the iron industry were rarely smooth. The industry was very volatile and when it entered periods of depression then tensions ran high. Employers were keen to impose a high level of discipline evidenced by the rules at John Bradley's ironworks around 1820. Of the eighteen rules, thirteen stipulated the fines to be incurred if they were broken and others carried the threat of prosecution or dismissal.[251]

We have no record of the rules in any of the Rose's ironworks but the first incident of note that we have illustrating David Rose's relations with his workforce comes in May 1852 and is quite a shocking one. *'A forgeman named John Eaton was fined £5 and costs for having violently assaulted his master, Mr David Rose, ironmaster, of Wednesbury. As Mr Rose was passing the furnace where the defendant was at work, on Monday afternoon, he observed a quantity of coal burning away in waste in the ash-hole, and on remonstrating with the defendant he was very abusive and struck him a violent blow on the head, which knocked him down and rendered him insensible. In default of payment, the defendant was committed for two months to hard labour.'*[252]

The tensions in the industry at that time were evident. In September 1852 a strike of puddlers at Bradley, Foster & Co. of Shutt End led to the prosecution of 39 puddlers on a charge of leaving their work. The men were given sentences ranging from a £2 fine to a month's imprisonment. In the iron industry it was the puddlers who had leverage with the managers. A puddler's job was skilled – they had the knowledge to determine when the puddling process was complete and the iron was malleable. If they went on strike then the ironworks shut down. Masters were well aware of this state of affairs and did their best to keep the puddlers under control. If they left work early without completing their required number of heats, masters prosecuted them in the magistrates' courts where they faced fines.

The physical demands of the puddlers' job were immense. Elihu Burritt describes puddling at the Bromford Works of Messrs. Dawes in Oldbury. *'To an outsider looking into one of those sixty furnaces, and seeing, if his eyes would bear it, the boiling, bubbling mass of metal, ten times more than red hot, a puddle would sound too wet and watery to describe it. The puddlers who fish in the troubled fountain, are generally stripped to the waist, and flooded with perspiration. They fish out a mass at the end of the rod, of a weight which shows what athletes they are trained to be. I hardly know what figure to use to convey an idea of the appearance and consistency of this burning, frittering, fizzy mass of metal thus brought out of the furnace.'*[253]

The physicality of the work and the intense heat shortened their active lives. Exposure to the heat of the furnaces was exacerbated during hot summers, as in 1871, when it was reported in the Iron Trade Circular that some works suspended production, 'for not even the trained English puddler can stand the fearful toil.'

251. Dudley Archives, The John Bradley Collection, D6
252. *The Staffordshire Advertiser*, 15th May 1852
253. Elihu Burritt, op.cit. p181-82

A strike in 1858 led to a discussion of what puddlers' wages ought to be. A sliding scale for pay was established, the Thorneycroft scale, which provided that puddlers' wages should vary with the official 'marked bar' prices at the rate of 1 shilling for every price change of £1 per ton. Other workers were to be covered by a rise of 10% in wages for every £1 increase in the price of iron per ton. The Puddlers' Protection Society was set up which accepted the scale.

The late 1850s and 1860s were a testing time for industrial relations in the iron industry. The main weapon that the employers used was the Master and Servant Acts which concerned breaches of contract or damage to property. Between 1858 and 1867 there were 10,000 prosecutions under these Acts in Staffordshire alone. There are a number of examples of how David Rose clashed with his puddlers.

The first one dates from September 1859 and illustrates how the Act was used. Henry Upton was charged *'with having neglected the service of Mr David Rose. It was an ordinary case of leaving without giving the necessary fortnight's notice; but the defendant said that he was discharged without notice by the complainant. In the course of the evidence it transpired that there had been some inducement used to influence the underhand, and that the furnaces had been stopped for several days.'* The prosecution asked for an exemplary punishment and Upton was sentenced to fourteen days imprisonment with hard labour.[254] Upton had a history of being obstructive. A year earlier he had featured in a dispute with Thomas Wells, another Moxley ironmaster when he refused to transfer from one furnace to another and left work without notice.[255]

The odds were weighted heavily in favour of the employer. If the employer was at fault then he was subject to a civil action and possible damages. If the employee was at fault then it was a criminal offence with a maximum sentence of three months. There was a long and bitter strike in 1863 at a time when the puddlers demanded an advance of a shilling a ton. Large firms like Hingley's and the British Iron Company led the way in prosecuting men under the Masters and Servants Acts for neglect of work or breach of contract. David Rose followed suit. The year was a busy one for prosecutions involving his puddlers. In February 1863 four puddlers including Eli Brant and William Evans were charged with neglect of service and fined 8 shillings and costs having *'put the firm to considerable expense.'*[256]

In April 1863 another four puddlers in David Rose's works - Richard York, Richard Stokes, Thomas Collins and Samuel Toon were also charged with neglect of service: *'York and Stokes, the two day hands, left work when they had finished the fifth heat, leaving one heat uncompleted. Collins and Toon, the two night hands, upon entering the works refused to charge the furnaces, and immediately left the premises.'* While York was discharged, pleading illness, the other three were fined ten shillings and costs.'[257]

In November 1863 William Hurlstone, a puddler, summoned David Rose for non-payment of 10 shillings wages. These had been withheld as a fine for failing to appear for work. Hurlstone claimed that he had been ill and had sent a note from the chemist but the case was adjourned until he could produce a certificate to verify his illness.[258]

254. *The Birmingham Daily Post*, 14th September 1859
255. *The Birmingham Daily Post*, 23rd December 1858
256. *The Birmingham Daily Post*, 26th February 1863
257. *The Birmingham Daily Post*, 9th April 1863
258. *The Birmingham Daily Gazette*, 25th November 1863

Sometimes the puddlers might have had just cause for their actions. Some iron was better to work than others and the extra labour and time needed led to many grumbles in the workplace. Iron made by hot blast was a particularly contentious issue as puddlers found this type more difficult to work. Workers in the iron industry, and the Rose factories in particular, were not simply fighting their own cause. Notices in the *Birmingham Journal* and *Birmingham Post* in March 1863 reveal their solidarity with the workers in other parts of the country. Contributions of £3 6s and then £5 were noted from the Rose workers in Moxley to the Cotton Districts Relief Fund in Lancashire.[259]

In the same period David's cousin, Thomas, was experiencing similar challenges in the Bilston area. Forty puddlers employed at his Millfields and Bradley Works gave notice of their intention to strike in support of men in the East Worcestershire District who were demanding a wage rise. Rose's puddlers had been making bar iron to supply the Earl of Dudley's Round Oak Works[260] and it was the Earl who was in dispute with the workers from East Worcestershire. There were also troubles with individual workmen in Thomas Rose's concern. In October 1863 Richard Beach was summoned for assaulting the manager at the Millfields Works for a delay in paying him the wages which he was owed when he gave notice to leave. Beach was found guilty, fined 20 shillings and given a month's imprisonment.[261]

At this point ironworkers across the country decided to form the National Association of Puddlers, Shinglers, Rollers and Millmen, which held its first conference at Brierley Hill in May 1864. There were 70 delegates representing 6,870 men. Pay was again on the agenda, together with mechanised puddling. The union was also a source of raising funds for workers in distress during strike periods. The puddlers' strike continued until August when the masters agreed to most of the terms since their order books were full. The masters, however, were intent on opposing further demands by the Association. They began to organise regionally in an attempt to break the union. This was a period when the iron trade was again beginning to stagnate, witnessed by the numerous bankruptcies over the next two or three years.

In 1865 there was another strike known as the 'Great Lock Out,' precipitated by a downturn in trade. To offset the impact of this downturn a resolution was drawn up in December 1864 and signed by many ironmasters including Daniel Rose and David Skidmore, William Rose, David Rose and Daniel Offley who agreed, *'to give fourteen days' notice of a reduction of one shilling per ton in puddling and 10 per cent in millmen's and other wages connected with forges and mills, on the 31st instant; and we do further agree, that in the event of the men in any works of the undersigned refusing to work, to give fourteen days' notice on the Saturday immediately following to close our works till all the men agree to return to their work.'*[262]

The puddlers in North Staffordshire reacted by striking and ironmasters determined upon a joint stance against them. A national meeting of ironmasters was held in February 1865 with representatives from the Middlesborough district, Lancashire, Yorkshire and Staffordshire. Amongst the firms present were those of David Rose as well as his brother

259. *The Birmingham Journal*, 7th March 1863; *The Birmingham Post*, 10th March 1863
260. *The Birmingham Daily Post*, 11th July 1863
261. *The Birmingham Daily Gazette*, 28th October 1863
262. *The Birmingham Journal*, 7th January 1865

Daniel and David's son-in-law, Daniel Offley. The representatives agreed to establish a National Association of the Iron Trade to counter the workers Association. After long discussions another resolution was drawn up and passed stating that, *'It having been officially announced that the strike of the puddlers in North Staffordshire has been directed by the executives of the Puddlers' Union, and it having been ascertained that weekly contributions are regularly being levied and paid for by the men employed in other districts in support of the strike, we the undersigned, do hereby agree that we will give fourteen days' notice on Saturday next, the 18th inst, to close our works, unless the men in North Staffordshire shall, before the expiration of this notice, have returned to work at the same reduction in wages as has been accepted in other districts. The notices will be given on Saturday and the works closed on the 4th of March. '*[263]

The lock-out was strictly adhered to at most of the large works including those of David Rose, his brother William and his cousin, Thomas.[264] In Bilston around 7,000 ironworkers were made idle. The consequences of this were soon felt by some of the poorest families. In March 1865 a meeting of the Puddlers' Union was held which listed the numbers of men entitled to relief. Amongst the places listed was Moxley, with 87 workers entitled to support. Some members were still at work and able to contribute to the support of the rest who were locked out.[265] However, in April the South Staffordshire men decided to end their action while those in North Staffordshire carried on. Yet it was an uneasy truce and in December puddlers from Thomas Rose's works were again convicted for neglect of work and in turn they gave notice to strike.[266]

The puddlers continued to play a pivotal role in the iron industry. Whereas during the 19th century the capacity of individual blast furnaces steadily increased, the puddling furnace was no larger than it had been in 1800 and an increase in output could only be achieved by building more furnaces and hiring more puddlers.

In January 1867 the puddlers determined to strike rather than accept lower wages because of the downturn in trade. A year later another cut was considered by some ironmasters. In March 1868 David Rose attempted to reduce the wages of his puddlers and millmen but failed because he was not supported by other masters.[267] By May 1868 the ironworkers were again on strike and a Central Strike Committee was formed with some of its members making a tour of the country to seek aid from other trade societies for the support of the strike. A handbill was issued to the iron-workers outlining the arguments on the non-necessity of reducing wages. These arguments ran along the lines that the men had suffered a 20% cut in wages over three years which had done little to revive the industry. The South Staffordshire men also objected to having to work at a common national rate of 7s 6d per ton since the quality of their iron was higher than that produced in the north of the country.[268]

Eventually the men went back to work but tensions still remained between masters and men, epitomised by a case concerning David Rose in January 1869. An engineer, Simeon Holland, employed by Rose at his Moxley works, was charged under the Masters and

263. *The Birmingham Daily Post*, 17th February 1865
264. *The Birmingham Daily Post*, 7th March; *The Birmingham Daily Gazette*, 13th March 1865
265. *The Manchester Courier*, 22nd March 1865
266. *The Sheffield Daily Telegraph*, 30th December 1865
267. *The Staffordshire Advertiser*, 7th March 1868
268. *The Birmingham Daily Post*, 16th May 1868

Servants Act with allowing a boiler to be without water causing £40 worth of damage. Holland argued that he was well aware of the dangers arising from allowing a boiler to lose water and that he had not turned on the blow-cock to allow water to escape. He was given a character reference by Mr Hazelhurst, the chief engineer, who testified that he had never known Holland to be guilty of negligence in the past. Despite this he was found guilty and fined £10 with costs.[269]

It was the wage question, however, which continued to dominate relations. In July 1870 the ironworkers pressed for an increase in their wages. Several meetings of ironworkers were held including one at Great Bridge which included delegates from David Rose's Albert Works, as well some from the Batman's Hill Works run by his brother William.[270]

While in the north of England a Board had been set up to resolve differences between masters and men, it was not so easy in Staffordshire. The Midland employers were not ready for anything so formal but in 1872 talks between the Ironworkers' Union and the Ironmasters' Association of South Staffordshire and East Worcestershire led to the setting up of the first South Staffordshire Iron Conciliation Board with 12 employers and 12 operatives. It was very informal with no rules and no president but a sliding scale was introduced and where difficulties arose in its operation the Board met to reconcile them.

Staffordshire workers in the boom of 1872 saw their wages rise by 20%. In this period the demand for higher wages was not restricted to the skilled ironworkers alone. In June 1872 carters and labourers from Wednesbury, Darlaston, Kings Hill, Great Bridge and Moxley, including men from David Rose's works, came together. They argued that, unlike the puddlers, they had not benefitted from wage rises. There was a demand for a union and a resolution that ironmasters should be given notice of a demand for an extra 6d a day.[271]

Relations were never easy and letters to local papers reflected the workers distrust. Their strength of feeling is reflected in letters to the *Birmingham Daily Post* in January 1873 in which it was argued that the masters never threw open their account books for the men to see whether they were being fairly treated on the sliding scale. Employers often apparently sent best iron to be worked at common iron prices. Other ironmasters were accused of not updating their puddling furnaces to save on the cost of fuel. In addition, repairs, fuel shortages and the like often prevented the men from working the usual five turns per week. It was also argued that he cost incurred by puddlers employing under-hands was not taken into consideration.[272]

One of the difficulties of the South Staffordshire Board was the inability of either side to control those whom they nominally represented. It broke down by the end of 1875 and the scale was abandoned.

The ironworkers' riot

As the iron industry in the Black Country began to suffer in the late 1870s and early 1880s, relations between masters and men declined rapidly. 1883 was a very hard time for trade. A wage reduction of 3d per ton was announced at the beginning of July and as a result a widespread strike ensued. It rapidly spread from West Bromwich and Smethwick to

269. *The Birmingham Daily Gazette*, 20th January 1869
270. *The Birmingham Daily Post*, 18th July 1870
271. *The Birmingham Daily Post*, 15th June 1872
272. *The Birmingham Daily Post*, 28th January 1873

Oldbury, Wednesbury, Darlaston, Tipton and the immediate districts. Strikers meetings were held and the situation became inflamed, *'a gang of men, about a thousand in number started off a procession, headed by a brass band with the avowed intention of causing the men at several works in the locality to lay down their tools.'*[273]

Two hundred men burst through the gates of Hatton's works at Bradley and intimidated the workers there. Men tried to storm the works of Tolley and Sons at Darlaston Green after a meeting was held at *The Fiery Holes* in Moxley, reputedly attended by 15,000 people. Further works were then attacked including those of David Rose. The next day thirteen men were brought before a special court at Wolverhampton Town Hall, including William Powell of Wednesbury who was charged with doing damage to the Rose's Moxley works and being about to pull bars out of the furnace.[274]

A second hearing was held two weeks later when a Samuel Pearson was also charged. It was estimated by Joseph Wall the manager of the Moxley works and Samuel Wright, a ball furnaceman, that £40 worth of damage was done. The desperation of the strikers and the enormity of what they had done was evidenced by Sergeant Given who testified *'to hearing Pearson crying in the cells at Wednesbury. Witness told him not to cry like that, and prisoner said, 'I'm very sorry for being at Rose's works. I never went there with the intention of doing any harm.' He went on, 'I never drew any of the bars but I got the firehook and raked the fire out of one of the furnaces, which I reckon they will think just as bad'.*[275]

By this time things had calmed down somewhat. The workers had wanted a rise of 6d per ton but the majority then backed down. Meetings of ironworkers were held in various locations and a vote was held on whether they should demand an advance in wages, go back to the old rate or accept a reduction. The men at David Rose's works voted: *'for the advance 38, the old rate 89 and a reduction, 1'*. Whether all the men voted we do not know, but the figures reveal that there were still at least 128 workers at David Rose's Moxley works in 1883.[276] The riot was the last significant unrest involving David Rose's works before his final bankruptcy three years later.

Mining unrest and the impact on David Rose's concerns
Labour unrest was not confined to David Rose's ironworkers. The colliery workers were also affected. The scenes witnessed above concerning the ironworkers' riot had been much more prevalent in the mining industry at an earlier date. In March 1855 at the time that David Rose had branched into mining operations with Richard Fletcher in Bilston, 500 miners marched from Bilston, through Portobello, Willenhall, Darlaston and Moxley visiting many pits and encouraging workers to join them. Their numbers swelled to about 3,000 who eventually surrounded 300 constables who had been tracking them, *'and the police had to make a vigorous use of the back of their weapons to escape – one of their number having been knocked senseless to the ground by a blow from a stone.'*[277] The crowd raided a grocer's shop and attacked an ironfounder, named Gettings, and his son while another policeman was stoned. All local shops closed. Five of the rioters were arrested and committed for trial at the assizes.

273. *The Midland Advertiser*, 7th July 1883
274. *The Birmingham Daily Post*, 7th July 1883
275. *The Birmingham Daily Post*, 27th July 1883
276. *The Midland Advertiser*, 21st July 1883
277. *The Morning Post*, 24th March 1855

The slump in the iron trade in the winter of 1857-58 again brought wage cuts, with the miners agreeing to a drop of 6d per day. In the following June wage reductions were again agreed upon in Tipton, Oldbury and West Bromwich. Those mining thick coal had their wages reduced from 5s to 4s a day and other coal miners went down to 3s. Miners east of Dudley refused reductions and went on strike. More strikes occurred in 1861 and 1863 and in that year the Miners' National Association was formed. In May 1864, following the reduction of wages to 3s a day, meetings of miners were held and a mass turn-out occurred. From August to the end of November a general strike paralysed the coal field. The miners' industrial action obviously had a knock on effect on the iron industry. Later in the decade we have occasional references to men from David Rose's mines attending as delegates to miners' conferences. These reports show that the miners concerns went far beyond wages.

In September 1869 a miners' conference was held at Dudley with fifty men in attendance representing some 22 collieries together with forty others. One man represented the colliers from David Rose's mine at Old Hill. The discussions covered all aspects of their work. High on the list was the move to limit the working day to 10 hours and it was agreed that a petition be presented to their employers. They complained about the evils of the charter-master system and that miners should be paid by the ton rather than the hour. There was also no consistency in the levy for sick pay with some paying 3 shillings and others 6 shillings. The Miners Association had £2,000 in the bank which they wished to be used as a widows and orphans fund and for men who were permanently disabled by their work. The men also voted to draw up a petition on safety in the mines insisting that the thick coal should always be worked with timber supports. In addition they called for more mine inspectors and education for the miners so that accidents could be avoided.[278]

In December 1871 the *Birmingham Daily Post* covered a meeting of colliery engine tenders, at Princes End near Tipton, which gives an insight into the working practices at the collieries. There was a representative from David Rose's Moxley pits. The meeting focussed on wages and the reluctance of the larger coal-masters to agree to a rate of 4 shillings per day and the need to petition them. The engine winders maintained that their work as men in operating winding engines involved great responsibilities and that they should oppose the tendency of mine owners using banksmen and other colliers to man the engines. One delegate spoke against the overtime system and that it should be banned since most of the accidents happened during that time. There was a feeling that if they worked on a Sunday then their wage rate should be increased.

It was agreed that all these points be included in a petition to the coal-masters. A delegate from Moxley announced, amidst applause, that the winders at Rose's colliery had given their notices in, and they would expire on the following Saturday. Rose had offered them 2d extra per day, but this had been refused. The same delegate rejoiced that they had formed an association, and that many had joined.[279]

Barnsby in his 'Social Conditions in the Black Country' argues that the development of trade unionism among colliery enginemen was an example of a union set up to deal with a grave social evil just as much as it was to obtain improved wages. The enginemen were concerned with two problems. One was safe winding in the pit and the second was the safety of the boiler which the enginemen were responsible for. There was a general tendency to put young and inexperienced persons in charge of boilers in mines and ironworks. It may

278. *The Birmingham Daily Gazette*, 7th September 1869
279. *The Birmingham Daily Post*, 11th December 1871

be relevant that an accident had occurred the year before at David Rose's works involving a young boy in charge of a boiler. As early as 1859 HG Longridge the Black Country Mines Inspector had reported that boys as young as eleven were put in charge of engines.

By March 1872, miners had begun to press for a nine hour day and it appeared that by April 1872 that the dispute was coming to an end. *The Birmingham Daily Post* reported that several colliery masters, including David Rose, had agreed to a nine hour day for the engine tenders. However, the dispute was still around two months later in June. Another meeting of the colliery engine tenders was held at Kings Hill near Darlaston and among the pits represented was, again, David Rose's Moxley Colliery. Whether David Rose had agreed to the nine hours at Old Hill but not at Moxley, we do not know, but more likely, the Moxley winders were pushing for an increase in wages as well as a decrease in hours. A resolution was passed to give a fortnight's notice to the employers of their intention to strike unless a nine hour day and a daily rate of 4 shillings was agreed to.[280]

The mood of the miners seems to have been particularly bullish as their demands spread to other areas and a further reduction of hours to eight a day. A meeting of miners at Darlaston was convened in July 1872 in response to the employers and chartermasters proposing that one hour a day be set aside for meals. The chartermasters had proposed that the men should begin at 7am, have an hour's dinner time and finish at 4pm. The colliers themselves wished to start at 6am, have no dinner time and finish at 2pm.[281]

A year later the agitation amongst the colliery engine tenders was still in evidence. A big meeting was held at Kings Hill in March 1873 and again David Rose's Moxley pits were represented. Again there was a call for a wage increase.[282] However in 1873, trade began to take a downturn with the onset of the Great Depression which was to ultimately bring down many firms including that of David Rose. The 8 hour day was under attack from the onset from the mine owners. A meeting in Darlaston in 1874 of miners' delegates discussed how employers were raising hours to nine, and coal and beer allowances were being withdrawn.

A miners' strike occurred in 1874 and lasted for 4 months. In June of that year *The Birmingham Daily Post* reported on the state of the strike in South Staffordshire and the power of the union. No mention is made of miners in Moxley but the article does refer to small pits and reports that many of the miners there had gone back to work. However, the strike was resolved with the masters being forced to sit around a table and a sliding scale of wages was agreed, tying them to the price of coal. This led ultimately to a drop in wages as the Depression deepened.[283]

In October 1874 wages for miners were 4s 6d per day but by 1882 they were 2s 4d. The result was that there was ever present dissatisfaction amongst the miners and their tendency to strike had a knock-on effect on the iron industry with pig iron production in the area being halved. By this time the Black Country iron industry, faced with increasing competition from other parts of the country, was in decline. The miners may have been digging their heels in but the downward spiral continued and the prospects of the workforce in both industries began to deteriorate.

280. *The Birmingham Daily Post*, 12th June 1872
281. *The Birmingham Daily Post*, 8th July 1872
282. *The Walsall Observer*, March 1873
283. *The Birmingham Daily Post*, 13th April 1876

14. The impact of the Rose concerns on the landscape: clashes with local authorities

While ironworkers and miners continued to work in life-threatening conditions and were struggling to maintain their income, their families faced increasing physical hazards from the impact of both those industries. As early as 1848 the *Mining Journal*, describing the rapid development of the Black Country, referred to *'heaps of ashes, semi-mountains of 'spoil' from the mines, with pools of stagnant water at their intersections, dense masses of smoke from the open coke fires, the engine houses, and the ironworks, and sulphurous streams of steaming water ...'*[284]

David Rose's concerns contributed to this environmental catastrophe in several ways. David Rose's Albert Works had diversified into galvanising in the mid-1860s and may have been the subject of a complaint lodged to the Bilston Commissioners in 1866 by the clergy and other inhabitants of Moxley, *'who find the smoke from a certain ironworks offensive and injurious.'*[285] The first specific mention we have comes in March 1870 at a meeting of the Wednesbury Board when, *'The Chairman read a letter which he had received from Mr D. Boaz, Moxley, who complained that his tenants were inconvenienced, and their health affected by Mr Rose's galvanizing works ... On the suggestion of the Chairman, the Clerk was directed to write to Mr Rose on the subject.'*[286]

A letter from the Board needed to be taken seriously. The Walsall Board had appeared to take a lead in this area as in January 1860 when they enacted a bye-law requiring proprietors of factories to control the emission of smoke.[287] In June 1869 they ordered the closure of the galvanising operations of Messrs Longmore and Lees, their decision being supported by a letter from 140 rate payers.[288]

Pollution from galvanising was not the only problem. In May 1874 David Rose was informed that *'he had rendered himself liable to heavy penalties for having proceeded with the erection of an engine stack without first laying plans before the Board, and that the stack must be carried up to the prescribed height of 60 feet.'*[289]

In addition to that there were other environmental concerns which the Board of Health raised. The operation of David Rose's railway sidings were discussed at the same meeting when the clerk reported that he had not sent an acceptance of the conditions under which the Board would allow him to run his locomotive engine across the road at Moxley. *'He was instructed to write again, informing Mr Rose that before he commenced running the engine he must signify in writing his intention to keep a man stationed at the crossing to stop the engine for the convenience of passengers, and to keep the rails at the level of the road.'*[290]

The second letter from the clerk obviously had an effect for at the next meeting of the Board the clerk reported that David Rose had accepted the conditions stipulated. David was

284. *The Mining Journal*, 17th June 1848
285. *The Birmingham Journal*, 20th October 1866
286. *The Birmingham Daily Post*, 2nd March 1870
287. *The Birmingham Daily Post*, 11th January 1870
288. *The Birmingham Daily Post*, 20th February 1877
289. *The Birmingham Daily Post*, 7th May 1874
290. *The Birmingham Daily Post*, 7th May 1874

obviously concerned that if he didn't comply then the Board might step in and close down a vital part of his transport network.

However it was the subject of roads which generated the most controversy. The saga began in September 1855 when Rose complained about the amount of money he had received for giving up land in Bull Lane. The Board refused to budge and David refused their cheque for £5 10s.[291] Two months later in November 1855 the matter was again discussed after a recommendation from a committee member that the sum be increased to £20. Again the Board declined.[292]

Eight years later, in May 1863, the roads were again a bone of contention. A delegation, including David Rose, John Wells, another ironmaster, and the local vicar petitioned the Board to award them £20 towards a cost of a watering cart which they would purchase so that the local Wolverhampton to Birmingham Road, which ran through Moxley, could be watered. However, the Board had no jurisdiction over the highway and the deputation was advised to approach the Bilston trustees.[293]

The deputation had argued that they received little benefit from their sizeable contribution to Local Board rates. However, the damage to the roads was often caused by the local coal and ironmasters themselves who were held to account by the Board. In August 1863 it was reported that David Rose had repaired Bull Lane which had been damaged by his mining operations.[294] The quality of work was obviously questionable since in early 1864 the Board's Surveyor reported that David Rose had promised to put the same road into a proper state of repair.[295] This was an ongoing issue - in September 1868 a report by the local Streets and Sewerage Committee called attention to the state of Moxley's roads which had been affected by subsidence caused by mining operations. The clerk was instructed to write to the relevant mine owners and inform that they should repair the roads immediately or else the commissioners would do so and charge them with the expense.[296]

The issue was obviously not resolved for in 1875 the surveyor for the Wednesbury Local Board, *'reported that the road at Moxley, by Bull's Lane, was in a more dangerous state than ever, and that Mr Rose and Mr Lowe each threw the blame upon the other. Mr Marson and Mr Joseph Taylor each added a few words as to the extremely dangerous state of the road. The clerk was instructed to take proceedings against Mr Rose and Mr Lowe to remedy the evil complained of.'*[297]

Sanitation

The impact that pits had on the sanitation of the area is illustrated by a meeting of the Board of Guardians at Walsall in 1865 when, *'Mr Green referred to the probability of an outbreak of cholera occurring in this country, and advocated the taking of every possible precautionary measure to prevent the spread of that epidemic. He stated that large tracts of ground having subsided in the neighbourhood of Darlaston from the working of the mines beneath, the hollow had become filled with sewage matters from Bilston and water from the*

291. *The Staffordshire Advertiser*, 8th September 1855
292. *The Staffordshire Advertiser*, 17th November 1855
293. *The Staffordshire Advertiser*, 9th May 1863
294. *The Staffordshire Advertiser*, 29th August 1863
295. *The Birmingham Daily Post*, 14th January 1864
296. *The Staffordshire Advertiser*, 19th September 1868
297. *The Birmingham Daily Post*, 17th November 1875

canal, the accumulations giving out most noxious gases in warm weather, and seriously endangering the health of the inhabitants. The Darlaston Board of Surveyors had written to the owners of the pits in question asking them to remove the nuisances complained of ... '[298]

An earlier report of 1843 documented the effects of ironworking on Darlaston's water supply: *'Bronchocele and calculous diseases are prevalent, which is attributed to the water of the neighbourhood being impregnated with salts of lime and ironstone.* '[299] The result of all this was that Darlaston had one of the highest death rates of any town in the Black Country in the period 1840 to 1870.

Housing Conditions

The mortality rate in this period was also due to the appalling housing conditions in the area. The Roses had built dwellings for their workers as evidenced by census records which list 'Rose Buildings' as well as 'Skidmore Buildings' which housed families of miners as well as ironworkers.[300] The provision of housing for skilled workmen was a long-established tradition in the eighteenth century particularly in rural communities. These were generally of a good standard but in a more urban environment with a dense population, this was not the case.

Blakemore's Lane, Darlaston in the late 19th century, showing dilapidated housing conditions.
(By photographer John Aston, Courtesy Walsall Local History Centre)

298. *The Birmingham Daily Post*, 26th August 1865
299. 1843 Parliamentary Commission on the Employment of Children; Report by RH Horne
300. 1871 Census for Darlaston

Letters to the *Birmingham Post* in August 1866 describe some areas of Darlaston: '*In Bilston Street there is a yard where pigs are kept close to a bakehouse and where their filth dribbles down the unpaved yard, towards a dwelling house; and there is another open court, where the privy and ashpit adjoin a small nailmaker's shop in which half a dozen people are constantly at work, and where the cesspool is in a bad condition ... Coming up to Cramp Hill, we turn into a court behind the police station, where there is a frightful pest-pool. Three privies empty into it, and it lies open to the day; a reeking, yellow and green liquid mass that ought, if it did its appointed work, to spread fever through Darlaston ...*'

Housing conditions in Woods Bank, where David Rose had one of his collieries, were shocking. At a meeting of the Darlaston Local Board in January 1875, '*The Medical Officer reported an exceptionally high death-rate, due mainly to the severity of the weather, twenty-three deaths having occurred from diseases of the respiratory organs, against three from zymotic diseases. Smallpox had shown itself in several houses at Woods Bank, and one case in the Old Gardens. All these were convalescent ... One of the cases, which had proved fatal, occurred at No 18 Woods Bank, a small back house, consisting of one lower room and one sleeping room, with no back door and no ventilation.* '[301]

Deaths could arise from attempts by the poor to cure the aliments that afflicted their families. One such case involved the death of six year old John Vann, the son of a roller employed by Daniel Rose. An inquest held in September 1863 focussed on whether the chemist, a Mr Woolley, had supplied laudanum instead of a tincture of rhubarb to treat the boy's stomach ache. The case was adjourned while an analysis of the content of the boy's stomach was carried out. We have no record of the final outcome.[302]

301. *The Birmingham Daily Post*, 6th January 1875
302. *The Grantham Journal*, 5th September 1863

15. Individual responses of workers to their living conditions

Charles Thornhill, the local surgeon, commented in typical Victorian fashion on the habits of working people in the Darlaston area: *'The women here of the working classes are very prolific, many of them having a child every year. It is a common thing here for a woman to have nine to twelve children. The number of illegitimate children is great, many of the girls having had three to four each ... The improvidence and want of management among the working classes is very great; they are extravagant as possible whenever they get the means; many of them will have large joints of meat on Sundays and the earlier part of the week, and be in almost a starving condition by Friday and Saturday; there is much drunkenness here in the early part of the week when trade is good; the women are great smokers.'*[303]

While some of the above may well have been true, the habits of the workers were moulded by the uncertainty of their income as well as their dreadful housing and sanitary conditions. The following cases look at some of the ways that the Roses' employees reacted individually to these conditions. Some sought parish relief, others emigrated. Some committed assault or resorted to murder while others vandalised property. While stealing was commonplace some just gave up trying to support their families.

The plight of a puddler seeking relief

Workers had few options when times became hard. One was to take industrial action. Another was to seek relief. We get an idea of the consequences of the depression on the families in the area from an article in the *Birmingham Journal* in February 1858 when thousands of ironworkers in the area had been thrown out of work. The paper reports that 150 half gallons of soup had been distributed by a local Bilston committee. A more structured approach came in the form of Poor Law provision. During the slump in the mid-1860s one of David Rose's workers applied for relief to the Wolverhampton Board of Guardians. The frustration that he and his fellow workers felt at not being able to practice their trade is evident from the report that: *'The majority of the applicants were underhand puddlers, labourers, miners and also one puddler, the first of the latter class who has yet applied here. He stated that he had been employed at the works of Mr David Rose, Bradley, until the works closed, and in answer to the Chairman said he did not belong to the Workman's Union. They all expressed their regret at having to take to such a job as stone breaking.'*[304]

Violent assault: Joseph Lewis

One of the earliest examples of what desperate measures some of the Rose workers resorted to occurred in 1857 when Daniel Rose's works manager came close to death. The period was again one of economic uncertainty although it is unclear if this was behind the actions of Joseph Lewis, a hammerman at the Bull's Bridge Works. Lewis was charged with: *'stabbing Police-constable George Hague with a dagger, a formidable weapon, about six inches in length, and which presented the appearance of a Turkish scymetar in miniature.'*

Lewis had gone to the house of Mr John Page, the manager of Daniel Rose's works, and demanded wages that were not due to him. Page told him that if any wages were due he

303. The Children's Employment Commission, 1843. Evidence given by Charles Thornhill, no.237
304. *The Wolverhampton Chronicle*, 29th March 1865

should come to the office and his private residence. Lewis then became threatening and drew the knife and the police were called. The officer, George Hague, told the accused that if he had any claim against Page then he must take legal steps to enforce it. Lewis then stabbed the constable three times before being eventually handcuffed. The surgeon testified that had the dagger penetrated further then the consequences would have been serious. Lewis was committed for trial at the next assizes.[305]

Murder: The Lloyd case

In May 1871 an inquest was held on the murder of a Mrs Lloyd by her husband. The Lloyds had recently moved to Darlaston and William Lloyd was employed as a puddler in David Rose's Victoria Works in Moxley. Apparently the 35 year old Lloyd had slept all day after working a night shift and then attacked his wife with a knife and a poker. Mrs Lloyd ran into the yard while her husband waved the 2½ foot long poker at the neighbours and threatened to kill them. As the neighbours retreated, Lloyd caught up with his wife and began to batter her about the head, hitting her over and over again until her skull was smashed.

The inquest revealed that the couple had been married for sixteen years. They had only been living in their cottage in Timmins Yard for over a week and Hannah George, their immediate neighbour, had gathered from Mrs Lloyd that her husband had not worked much in the previous twelve months. His son testified that both he and his father had worked a shift at Rose's factory and then returned home to bed. He heard his father praying and crying in another room. He also testified that his father had once knocked out one of his mother's teeth when she asked him to leave a public house and go home. Lloyd had also lost his head and threatened his wife with a poker on another occasion the previous Christmas and said he would shoot her. On that occasion he was attended by three doctors. The son said that on the night before the murder his father had not been drinking and did not drink much because he was prone to fits.[306]

Lloyd was charged with murder but found not guilty by reason of insanity. One wonders what tipped him over the edge – was it something that had happened at Rose's works?

Neglect: The Essock case

In February 1872 another case was reported which was even more shocking, concerning Joseph Essock who was charged with deserting his children. Essock was employed at David Rose's works in Moxley and lived in Mill Street, Ryecroft with his wife and children. His wife had been expecting another child and had been attended by both a parish nurse and the parish medical officer.

His wife had subsequently died while Essock was at work but when he returned home on the Saturday evening, instead of staying with his children, he locked them in with the corpse and went to the pub where he drank until he was intoxicated. The pattern was repeated on the Sunday and on Monday he went away but did not go to work. The same day some of the neighbours discovered that the children were in the house with the body. The police arranged for the children to be removed to the Workhouse and arrested Essock.

Essock was charged with both desertion and with wilfully causing the death of his wife through neglect and ill-treatment. The court heard that Police Constable Chell had found

305. *The Walsall Free Press & General Advertiser*, 1857
306. *The Birmingham Daily Post*, 6th May 1871

the three children aged seven, three and six weeks in a room in the cottage. The baby lay tied on a chair before the fire and was in a filthy condition. In another room he discovered the body of Mrs Essock lying on a mattress under a cover. The body was very thin and the smell was so bad that he had to leave. The only food in the house was a little butter and sugar. In a back room there was a filthy bag on the floor which the children said was their bed.

The cause of Mrs Essock's death was destitution and neglect. In his defence Essock said that he had asked for help from his wife's sister and father but they did not respond. The Medical Officer testified that he had previously offered to admit the family to the Workhouse but Essock refused. The prisoner was remanded for a week.[307] We have no record of the outcome of the case.

For the sake of a few pence: Samuel Stokes

Some employees found other ways to try and cut expenditure. On June 28th 1858 the *Birmingham Gazette* reported on the death of Samuel Stokes, a former employee of the Roses who was found lying dead on the line of the Great Western Railway, between Wednesbury and Bilston. It transpired in the course of the enquiry that Stokes was in the constant habit of boasting how he could cheat the railway companies, and that he had been fined the previous November for riding in a superior class carriage to the one he was entitled to use.

In this instance he had bought a ticket from Birmingham to Hockley but had carried on towards Bilston and *'when the speed of the train was slackened on approaching Bilston Station, he took the opportunity of jumping from the steps on the offside of the carriage, and was immediately knocked down by an up goods train which was then passing.'*[308]

Cases of theft

The most common response to poverty was resorting to theft. A number of cases occur where the Roses' workers stole from their employers. Woods describes the attitudes of the period. 'Taking home' was regarded as a customary right by the workers. In the Black Country many cases involved the stealing of basic raw materials such as coal, iron, tin, copper, lead and leather. As well as stealing from the work place, the tradition of 'coal-picking' was accepted as legitimate by these communities. Coal on the pit bank was regarded as a community asset and it was the women and children who were mainly involved in its appropriation. There was a sense of 'natural justice' attached to industrial theft which may have been a reaction to low wages, short time working or the truck system.[309]

Generally, the penalties for stealing from an employer were harsher than if the offence had been committed by an outsider because it was also an abuse of trust. Although employer-magistrates would not sit in cases particularly affecting them, their fellow magistrates would reflect their views. However, this trend was not always reflected in the cases brought against Rose employees. The first case involving one of David Rose's employees involved a young woman named Ann Talbot who worked in his brickyard. She

307. *The Birmingham Daily Post*, 21st February 1872
308. *The Birmingham Gazette*, June 25th 1858
309. DC Woods, 'Customary Rights and Popular Legitimation: Industrial Stealing in the Victorian Black Country'

'appeared in court on a charge of stealing a piece of coarse cloth, valued at 2d, from her employer. She came to work on the Monday wearing an apron she had repaired using the material she had stolen and was accused of theft by the manager of the brickyard.

Employees obviously had to provide their own work-clothes. Although she was arrested, David Rose did not want her to be heavily punished and she was eventually discharged, having already been in custody for three days.'[310]

A second case occurred in May 1869 when two boatmen, Henry Cope and John Poston were charged with stealing a bag of corn worth 4 shillings. *They were followed to*

Coal picking near Bilston Road, Wednesbury, 1897.
(Courtesy Sandwell Community History & Archive Service)

310. *The Birmingham Daily Post*, 21ˢᵗ April 1864

Birmingham and then apprehended, the stolen corn being found in the boat. The Stipendiary expressed his reluctance to stamp the prisoners – who had previously borne a good character – as felons and said that he would therefore assume that they merely unlawfully took the corn for the use of their master's horses, and not with a view of selling it for their own benefit.' Despite this, he still saw it as his duty to treat it as a serious offence and both men were given the option of paying a £5 fine or being imprisoned for two months.[311]

The greatest amount of industrial theft was that of coal-stealing and this was generally carried out by women and juveniles. In coal and iron communities, such as those around Darlaston, Wednesbury and Moxley, this offence was regarded by many as legitimate, particularly as great quantities of coal were simply lying around for the taking. In case after case before Black Country courts the defendants denied they had stolen the coal but had merely 'picked' it. Many coal owners pressed for heavy sentences because of the deterrent effect, realizing the almost impossible task of guarding all the pit banks.

However, this was not always so and a case in March 1858 involving Daniel Rose and his partner David Skidmore perhaps reveals the differing attitudes of the Rose brothers. *'John Massey was charged with stealing about 60lbs of coal from a pit bank, at Bilston, the property of Messrs Rose and Skidmore. The prisoner asserted that he worked at the pit and that his butty had given him permission to take the coal. Police Constable Hague stated that he took the prisoner into custody at the request of Mr Skidmore. Mr Skidmore did not appear against the prisoner, who was discharged, there being no evidence against him.'*[312] In this case the magistrate even rebuked the policeman for making the arrest without witnessing the crime!

There are many more instances of non-employees resorting to stealing from the Rose concern. In these cases harsher punishments do seem to have been the norm, particularly where the theft of iron itself was concerned. In July 1869 Benjamin Aston, a puddler, was accused along with three others by the names of Tyrer, Price and Bull of stealing twelve and a half hundredweight of pig iron from David Rose. The men were apparently engaged in dredging part of the canal near Rose's wharf in Wednesbury. Hemmings, the night-watchman, went to investigate and found that they had removed a quantity of iron. After challenging them he sought help but when he returned they had disappeared, leaving the boat and the iron. The men were sentenced to nine months' imprisonment with hard labour.[313]

In March 1870 Thomas Beech, a one-eyed scrap dealer, and his fifteen year old son, John, were charged with stealing six hundredweight of iron, valued at £3 10s. The two were seen with a horse and cart on a private road from part of David Rose's colliery where the foundations of an engine had been laid. The cart was found to contain plates from this foundation. The father ran off leaving the son to face the music. Both the accused were committed for trial but the son refused to implicate his father and was sentenced to six months' imprisonment.[314]

311. *The Birmingham Daily Post*, 5th May 1869
312. *The Birmingham Journal*, 27th March 1858
313. *The Staffordshire Sentinel and Commercial & General Advertiser*, 24th July 1869
314. *The Birmingham Daily Gazette*, 2nd March; *The Staffordshire Advertiser*, 5th March; *The Staffordshire Sentinel and Commercial & General Advertiser*, 9th April 1870

In August 1870 Thomas Kelly, alias Gilroy, a rag and bone man, was accused of stealing fourteen iron bands belonging to David Rose as well as 43 sheets of tin from elsewhere for which he received three months' imprisonment.[315] In January 1875 Alfred and John Handley stole a boat from David Rose's wharf. The men had negotiated with a dealer in Monmore Green to sell the boat. Their attempts to erase the boat's registration with the Birmingham Canal Company from the helm aroused suspicions and led to their arrest. Both were sentenced to six months' hard labour.[316]

These punishments pale into insignificance in comparison to the sentence handed down to two men charged with stealing two brasses from the engine house in Thomas Rose's works in 1856. One man, 20 year old Michael Dolan, was given a year's imprisonment with hard labour. The other, William Buckley, with a previous conviction, was sentenced to four years' penal servitude.[317]

Another case of theft from David Rose's works was reported in May 1877 when, at Wednesbury Police Court, Ellen Wentlin, aged seventeen was charged with stealing a quantity of iron from a truck. On this occasion, David Rose declined to press the case and the prisoner was discharged but had to pay costs.[318]

Persistent theft, however, was punished heavily. On June 25th 1882 Thomas Hartshorne of Darlaston was accused of stealing coal from a marl hole on David Rose's property. *'About two boat loads of coal had been missed recently, and prosecutors asked that the prisoner should be made an example of. As he had been convicted several times previously, he was committed to the Sessions for trial.'* Hartshorne was sentenced to six months imprisonment.[319]

Even children were brought before the courts. In March 1863 ten year old Mary Rooney was charged alongside Maria Marshall and Mary Ann Bamford with stealing two hundredweight of coal from Rose & Skidmore's Moorcroft Colliery. The offence was proved but the complainants declined to press the case.[320] In 1882 eight year old James Bird was charged with stealing iron from the works of David Rose & Sons at Moxley. The boy said that there were other lads who had taken iron to sell to 'John the Ragman.' What happened to James is not recorded.[321]

When times were particularly hard some people resorted to stealing food. In October 1861 it was reported that a thief had been apprehended in David Rose's garden at Cockheath and that garden robberies in the area had been increasing in frequency with fruit and vegetables being stolen.[322]

Forgery

Some men resorted to using counterfeit coin. In April 1858 James Brown and Joseph Pritchard were brought before the courts for such a crime. The two men were both in the employ of the Roses, Brown having worked at Moxley as a waggoner for eleven years.

315. *The Staffordshire Advertiser*, 20th August 1870
316. *The Birmingham Daily Post*, 1st January 1875
317. *The Staffordshire Sentinel and Commercial & General Advertiser*, 8th March 1866
318. *The Birmingham Daily Gazette*, 16th May 1877
319. *The Darlaston Weekly Times*, June 25th; *The Birmingham Daily Post*, 27th June 1882
320. *The Birmingham Daily Post*, 26th March 1863
321. *The Darlaston Weekly Times*, 1882
322. *The Birmingham Daily Post*, 1st October 1861

They were accused of having attempted on two occasions to buy ale using a counterfeit florin. Both men were remanded in custody while the court contacted the Mint to pursue their prosecution.[323]

Vandalism

Other young men took out their frustrations through vandalism. In September 1863 Thomas Owen, a young collier who had recently been imprisoned for damaging skips at one of the Rose's collieries, was sentenced to three months for a similar offence at Willingsworth Colliery.[324] Sometimes the vandalism was committed by employees. In May 1864, a young man named Baugh, employed in Thomas Rose's Millfield Works, inserted bars of iron into the mechanism of a steam engine in a deliberate attempt to sabotage it. This was his second such offence and he was sent to prison for a month.[325]

Emigration

A more drastic solution was to emigrate. A committee was formed in the Midlands in 1865 to encourage emigration to the United States as a result of the ongoing strike and depression in the iron trade.[326] In the late 1860s Wednesbury itself became the focal point of a collective decision to seek a better life abroad. The instigator of the scheme was a Father George Montgomery, the leader of a 3,000 strong Irish Roman Catholic community which had developed in the area following the Irish Famine. Montgomery raised money for the building of St Mary's Church but, shocked by what he considered to be the miserable and amoral state to which his parishioners had descended, he saw it as his duty to play a central role in community life. He saw that central to the problems experienced by his largely Irish flock was the fact that employment was always insecure and living conditions were harsh. Montgomery even petitioned Pope Pius IX for help, writing that: *'our temporal condition is entirely at the disposal of persons who have no relation to us but that of employers, who, so far as we are concerned, using their money only to make more money, hire us to work, or dismiss us to idleness, as their interests require.'*[327]

There was also the issue of sectarian strife. Irish residents were victimised in retaliation for nationalist activities and Irish Catholics in Wednesbury felt particularly vulnerable to attacks during periods of economic depression when they could become the scapegoats for economic misery. It is against this background of poverty, insecurity and religious and ethnic strife that Montgomery determined to encourage migration to a Catholic country, one where the Irish would enjoy protection, security of faith and morals.

He considered Brazil to be the ideal destination for poor catholic emigrants for *'in its immense territory and its teeming soil, Brazil has the means to sustain twenty times its present population'*. He praised the Brazilian emperor as being a compassionate and truly enlightened leader who was offering: *'the poorest strangers a welcome such as a nation never gave'*. Montgomery contacted Joaquin Maria de Almeida Portugal, the 'London representative of the Commercial Agency of Brazil', who in November 1867 had placed his first advertisements in English papers promoting Brazilian emigration. The terms were very generous and offered free passage. Word rapidly spread in Wednesbury and beyond of

323. *The Staffordshire Advertiser*, 24th April 1858
324. *The Staffordshire Advertiser*, 22nd September 1866
325. *The Huddersfield Chronicle*, 21st May 1864
326. *The Hull Packet*, 24th March 1865
327. Montgomery's Register, vol.1. no. 6, 19th October 1867

Montgomery's plan and he claimed that he had so many enquiries that he decided to organise two groups drawn only from the area.

On 3rd February 1868, hundreds of Brazil-bound emigrants began assembling at Wednesbury's London and North Western Railway Station. Of the group, 247 people were recruited in Wednesbury by Montgomery while the other 92, also mainly Catholics, were recruited mainly in Birmingham and London. Oliver Marshall[328] has compiled an incomplete list of the names of some of the emigrants which included James Shannon, an iron furnaceman living in West Bromwich, John Shannon a furnace labourer from Bilston as well as three men from Wednesbury - Austin Orgill, an ironroller, Peter Kenny, an ironworks labourer and John Shaughnessy, a tap or cinder wheeler.[329] While we do not know where these men were employed, we do know that the party included the family of William Rose, David's nephew who had converted to Catholicism on his marriage.[330] William had been employed as a colliery clerk probably at one of Daniel Rose's mines and had presumably lost his position on his uncle's death.

The emigrants travelled to Liverpool and boarded the Florence Chipman, a steamship bound for Rio de Janeiro. Having docked there in April 1868 most of the party then travelled 130 kilometres down the coast to Itaji and 80 kilometres inland to the newly formed colony of Principe Dom Pedro. At Itaji they met some of the departing English settlers who warned them against proceeding further. Perhaps not wanting to believe what they were being told, and certainly without the financial means to return to Rio, let alone England, the Wednesbury party allowed themselves to be escorted to the colony. The colony was made up of a few administrative buildings, two large stores, a 'hotel', a butcher's shop, a bakery, a blacksmith's forge, a gristmill, sawmill, several houses and a tavern. Rough trails were beginning to open up the colony's hinterland, forest was being cleared and land planted.

All the settlements in the Itaji valley were prone to flash floods, but Principe Dom Pedro's situation, which was also near the Aguas Clara River, made it especially likely to meet disaster. The fate of one of the colonists in August 1868 was communicated in a letter written by Bridget Shaughnessy. 'My dear mother, I must let you know to my grief that my husband was drowned on the 3rd August. He was going for seeds, and had to pass a large river in a canoe or small boat, and it turned over and he was drowned … in four feet of water and then he was swept by the flood into a place that was eighteen feet in depth and they could not find him until his body rose in six days'.[331]

Even more devastating events were to come. In the middle of the night on 27th November 1868 the inhabitants of both Principe Dom Pedro and Brusque were suddenly awoken by torrents of water raging down into the valley from what were normally gentle mountain streams. For the previous five months it had rained virtually every day and the ground had become saturated. Bridges and livestock were swept away along with the roads and trails. The colony staggered on for several months but eventually all the party from the Black Country either made their way to the United States, Argentina or back to England like William Rose and his family.[332]

328. Oliver Marshall, *'English, Irish and Irish-American Pioneer Settlers in Nineteenth-Century Brazil'*, 2005
329. 1861 Census
330. Rose oral family history
331. *The Birmingham Daily Post*, 21st December 1868
332. For a full account of this see Oliver Marshall, op.cit

16. Life in David Rose's household

While many of his employees struggled honestly to make ends meet or resorted to other means, David Rose lived a life of luxury. His first family home was at Heath House in Moxley but by the mid-1860s he had moved to Goldthorn Court one of the newly built mansions on Goldthorn Hill on the outskirts of Wolverhampton.

Heath House, (furthest left) Cockheath, Moxley, home of David Rose.

(Courtesy of Mary Harding)

It was a substantial residence set in over seven acres of land including a lodge and a cottage.[333] In 1865 as he settled into his new home David advertised for 2,000 yards of good turf, suitable for a lawn.[334] We get a fascinating insight into the opulent contents of Goldthorn Court (and another unnamed residence) from a sale catalogue of July 1893 when David Rose's affairs were being settled. These included all brass French bedsteads, hardwood bedroom suites, mahogany, birch and painted maple chests of drawers, Brussels carpets, drawing room suites in walnut and inlaid rosewood, a mahogany dining table and dinner wagon, a mahogany Dickens writing table, a walnut sideboard and several bronze and marble clocks and ornaments. In addition there was a top of the range pianoforte by Collard and Collard together with some 'valuable ancient pictures.'[335]

The circles that the Roses moved in, and the fare that they ate, are well-illustrated by a report in 1858, on the opening of the Stafford Assizes at Wednesbury. 'D Rose' was in attendance which may have been either David or Daniel. Since 850 leading men of the

333. Wolverhampton Archives, DX -793/2
334. *The Birmingham Daily Post*, May 1865
335. *The Birmingham Daily Post*, 13th July 1893

Goldthorn Court (Courtesy Wolverhampton Archives Service)[336]

district were there then we can assume both brothers were present. This, remember was a time of depression in the iron and coal industries.

> *'There was a profusion of the most superb wines, including champagne ad libitum, mulled Chateau, margeau &c &c, supplied from the High Sheriff's cellars... The following is the bill of fare for one table, the other two tables having a similar supply: one boar's head, two galentines of turkeys, two roasted turkeys, four brace pheasants, four brace partridges, three couples roasted fowls, two four-quarters lamb, two hind-quarters lamb, three tongues, ornamented, two hams, ornamented; three raised pies, game; three pies of pressed beef; four lobsters on dishes, four dishes of prawns, two collared eels in aspic jelly, four veal and ham cakes in jelly, three dishes of potted meats, two tureens of oyster soup, two tureens of Julienne soup, five moulds of calves' foot jelly, five moulds of creams, five Swiss tourtes, five dishes of fancy pastry, tea, coffee, bread and butter, rolls &c. Extra dishes: three brace pheasants, three brace of birds, three couples of fowls, three pies, three lobsters, three prawns, and replenish of soup. On sideboard: one chine of beef, one round of beef, and one rump of beef.'*[337]

At least the High Sherriff, ironmaster Philip Williams, had awarded 1s 6d to each of his workmen and ordered the remains of the lunch to be distributed amongst them and the poor families of the district. The lunch was followed with a procession to Wolverhampton Station led by a cavalcade of eighty gentlemen and 116 closed carriages as well as many open vehicles. The streets were lined with spectators but no indication is given of what they thought of this or the flags, the firing of cannon and peeling of church bells.

336. Wolverhampton Archives, DX- 219
337. *The Birmingham Daily Post*, 9th March 1858

David was a man with expensive tastes. A postcard survives, sent from the Albert Works, to a German merchant staying at the Queen's Hotel in Birmingham, concerning an order of wine.

Family scandal: An upstairs downstairs romance

Yet David's family life was not all a bed of roses. Domestic harmony was shattered by his son David's marriage to one of their household servants. This liaison, and his father's attempts to thwart it, was periodically splashed across newspapers up and down the country for six years. It was a classic case of what happens when the worlds of upstairs and downstairs become romantically entangled. But the story also illustrates the lengths that David Rose would go to both protect his family's reputation and also save money. It demonstrates the very different world that David and his family lived in with visits to Wales, France and even Uruguay.

The affair first came to notice in October 1865 when David Rose Senior appeared in court charged with assaulting and illegally imprisoning his son. The saga, however, had started several months earlier. It is a little difficult to discern all the true facts since by the time the case came to court, David Junior appears to have decided that he had acted a little hastily in not only bringing a charge against his father, but also in marrying a servant.

David Junior had been at school until Christmas 1864 when he had just turned sixteen. The plan was that he would finish his education in Germany, but on returning home he began a relationship with one of the family's servants, Anne York, who was in her early twenties. In early August the couple travelled to Kenilworth via Birmingham, where they were married. At that point, David's brother Henry appeared, having ascertained the whereabouts of the young man. At first David was unwilling to return home but was persuaded by his brother, Henry, leaving Anne at Kenilworth. David Rose Senior was obviously horrified at what had taken place and saw all his plans for his son about to disintegrate. He arranged for David and Henry to go on a tour of Wales and, in the meantime, arrangements were made for young David to go to South America, with his father undertaking to invest up to £3,000 in a business venture. David Junior had misgivings and on learning that he would have to leave immediately he refused to go.

At this point he was dragged across the breakfast room by his hair by his father and brother and kicked and beaten with even his mother joining in. One of the Rose's household servants, Sarah Langford, who may well have assisted the elopement, testified that when the assault occurred she cried out that David was about to be murdered and was about to get help but was stopped at the door by two of David Rose's men, Green and Brooks, who were preparing to take David Junior away in a horse and trap. The young man was hauled upstairs and locked in his brother Henry's room and his clothes taken away. Because of David Junior's denial that an assault had taken place, the case against his father and brother was dismissed.[338]

Following the dismissal of the assault charge, David Junior was sent to Monte Video in Uruguay to work for a firm of merchants with which David Senior was acquainted. He returned to England in 1866 before again going abroad, returning in 1868 and then leaving again for France. During one of these visits home he saw his wife and informed her that David Senior would not consent to the couple living together. As a result of this Anne's

338. *The Birmingham Daily Post*; *The Birmingham Daily Gazette*, 11th October 1865

father, Levi York, instituted an action against David Rose Junior for the maintenance of his wife at the rate of £2 per week. A jury found that York was entitled to £1 5s a week and awarded him £225 to cover the period since the marriage. The Rose family's response, undoubtedly devised by David Rose Senior and his solicitor, was for David Junior to be declared bankrupt and thus be unable to pay.

This case came to court in June 1869. David Junior admitted to being present at the Old Hill Colliery but denied that he was employed as a clerk and maintained that he was not paid a salary but was maintained by his father. He deposed that when he had declared himself bankrupt he had handed over all his valuables – a silver watch, ring, gold chain and a gun which were worth about £15. The judge, however, dismissed the bankruptcy claim and ordered that David Junior should support his wife.[339] At this point David was sent to France to avoid being arrested for non-payment, only returning in December 1870 at the outbreak of the Franco-Prussian War.

The final chapter in the saga came in April 1871 when David Rose Senior engineered a case against Anne Rose nee York, which was reported in the *Birmingham Daily Post*. A Mrs Ann Grant testified that Anne Rose had come to live with her at Leabrook in Wednesbury and that she had seen her husband and Anne Rose in a compromising position in the kitchen. The husband refused to give evidence, Anne Rose's 'desertion' was thus proven and David Junior was not liable to pay maintenance.[340]

Political, social and religious life

While the newspapers gave much coverage to the behaviour of David Rose's youngest son, there is little evidence of his life in other areas such as politics. Political radicals were hardly to the fore in the ironmaster community. Ironmasters and their counterparts saw themselves as the bedrock of national prosperity, the source of Britain's greatness and the means of its defence. Most ironmasters counted upon the stability of a society ruled by a landed oligarchy in order to safeguard their trade and open up new colonial markets.[341] Socially and politically, ironmasters had more in common with land agents, surveyors and lawyers. Indeed, David Rose depended heavily on the expertise of his lawyer, William Duignan, and one of his sons, George, who entered the legal profession himself, married Duignan's daughter.

We do know that David and his sons supported the Liberals. Both of them sat on a committee to support the two Liberal candidates for West Staffordshire, Foley and Foster, in the run up to the 1868 election[342] with Henry Fullwood Rose chairing a party meeting at Wednesbury.[343] Henry Fullwood Rose was also a lieutenant in the Fourth Battalion of the Staffordshire Rifle Volunteers based at Bilston. David Rose supported the institution by presenting the corps with a challenge cup which was competed for bi-annually.[344]

339. *The Birmingham Daily Post,* 11th May 1869 & 21st June 1869
340. *The Birmingham Daily Post,* 28th July 1871
341. Richard Hayman, 'Ironmaking,' 2005
342. *The Birmingham Daily Post,* 31st October 1868
343. *The Birmingham Daily Post,* 4th September 1868
344. *The Birmingham Daily Post,* 13th August 1866; *The Staffordshire Advertiser,* 15th June 1867

Yet we do see a playful side to the family. In July 1863 Henry Fullwood Rose played at a cricket match at the Moxley Club between two elevens, as did two D Roses and an Offley. Two weeks later in another match between Moxley and Wolverhampton at the Merridale Ground, Wolverhampton, an Offley and a Rose were listed as part of the Moxley team.[345]

We have very little evidence of David Rose's religious beliefs but he appears to have been a firm supporter of the established church. That he was keen to be seen in such a light can be gathered first from his attendance at the consecration of Moxley All Saints Church in June 1851[346] and second from the report of a very generous donation made to the same institution three years later. *'On Trinity Sunday last an elegant silver chalice, of the Camden pattern, was presented to Moxley church, bearing the following inscription: 'The gift of Mrs Zibiah Rose, to Moxley parish church. Presented on Trinity Sunday AD 1854.'*[347]

George Rose pictured in FW Hackwood, 'Wednesbury Faces, Places and Industries, 1897

We know that David Rose and his sons, Henry and William, attended the inauguration of Moxley Parish Church's spire, clock and chancel window in June 1877. The Bishop of Lichfield gave the sermon on the text: 'The city that is set on a hill cannot be hid.' He referred to the melancholy sight of the rows of houses around every mine and factory in the district compared with the church towers which dominated places such as Lichfield and Shrewsbury. He warned people to beware of the material and utilitarian spirit of the age reflected in the grand houses of the rich. The rich were the idolators of the age who laid up treasures for themselves but were not rich unto God.[348]

We might wonder what David Rose made of the sermon, reflecting on nearly 50 years of building an industrial empire based on the sweat and toil of men and women who lived in those rows of houses around his mines and ironworks. The methods by which David Rose had laid up his treasures were soon to be called into question when he went bankrupt in 1881.

345. *The Birmingham Daily Post*, 9th July & 23rd July 1863
346. *The Staffordshire Advertiser*, 28th June 1851
347. *The Staffordshire Advertiser*, 17th June 1854
348. *The Birmingham Daily Gazette*, 28th June 1877

17. The 1881 and 1886 bankruptcies

The beginning of the decline and the leasing of the Moxley Ironworks

The boom of the early 1870s, when David Rose established his blast furnaces at Moxley, did not last for long. Pig iron production in the area reached 726,000 tons in 1871 but this was the last occasion when Black Country production passed 700,000 tons. Well into the 1860s the British predominance in iron manufacture was such that if British producers followed a sensible price policy they all could gain. But with the rise of foreign rivals this was no longer so. The USA had been one of the main markets but after their financial crisis of 1857 and imposition of high import duties, demand was reduced. These were unsettled times.

In May 1873 speculative panic developed in central Europe and spread to the USA. There was no general commercial crisis in Britain, where the story was one of sagging, punctuated by heavy failures. In 1874 another slump hit the iron industry and pig iron production dropped to its lowest point for a decade. The *Birmingham Daily Post* regularly listed the furnaces of the area which were in and out of blast. By May neither of the Rose furnaces was in blast and a valuation of £64,000 of the Albert and Moxley Works was made with a view to a sale but this fell through.[349]

There had been many warning signs for the Black Country iron industry, well before that. Pig iron production declined more rapidly than wrought iron. In 1856 the area produced 22% of the national total but by 1860 it was only 12%. The main cause of decline was the exhaustion of the more productive and the shallower seams of minerals, particularly ironstone. In 1860 it was calculated that local ores were sufficient for 40 years but this had been too optimistic. By 1866, the Black Country produced only 50% of the ironstone consumed by the local iron trade and 300,000 tons of pig iron was imported annually from Wales and Derbyshire in the early 1860s. As production costs increased Black Country blast furnaces were blown out. In South Staffordshire the number dropped from 114 in 1870 to 76 in 1875. Ironmasters were reluctant to invest capital in new plant and machinery perhaps because of the approaching exhaustion of local minerals.

In the light of the downturn in trade it was therefore somewhat fortunate for David Rose that in October1874 he was able to lease the Moxley Ironworks for seven years to Joseph Henry Chavasse, the then manager of the ironworks, and John Southan, a coalmaster of Codsall, at a rent of £500 per annum.[350]

The depression in the iron industry set in for five years with only an occasional increase in sales. Throughout this time surplus capacity and surplus production overhung the market with nearly a million tons in producers' hands by 1879. Wrought iron was even more badly hit particularly with the development of steel. By 1875 the replacement of iron rails by steel was well under way in Britain. Staffordshire's share of national pig iron production continued to fall. Cheap iron was coming into the district from other furnaces, which local ironmasters were finding it difficult to compete with. It was noted that in South Staffordshire, *'pig iron prices are not so firm, owing to the importation of pigs from other districts, which can be sold in South Staffordshire at several shillings per ton below the quotation for native mine iron.'*[351]

349. *The Birmingham Daily Post*, 9th September 1886
350. S.R.O. D1317/1/11/4/1
351. *The Bristol Mercury*, 13th February 1875

The years 1876 and 1877 marked another downturn in the iron trade for South Staffordshire pig iron makers with more furnaces being blown out including, once again, one of David Rose's in April 1876, when it was reported that, *'The make of pig iron has now been reduced from 12,000 to 6,000 tons per week, and the output of finished iron has been reduced to below one half the usual amount. The two furnaces which have just been blown out are waiting till the miners are prepared to work longer hours, and the current very heavy expenses of working the pits thereby largely reduced ...* '[352] The state of affairs is reflected in the fact that William Napoleon Rose resigned his membership of the Institute of Mechanical Engineers in December that year, having not paid his subscription!

During the next decade many ironmasters ceased furnace operations altogether either through bankruptcy or their own choice. By 1890 only 27 locations remained in the Black Country where pig iron was made. 1879 was the last year there is a record of both David Rose's furnaces being in blast. One casualty of the depression was David Rose's brother, William who was declared bankrupt in December 1878 with liabilities in the region of £20,000.[353]

The galvanising side of David Rose's operation, however, was still going strong, with adverts being placed for both a foreman and a clerk who had expertise in that area.[354] Indeed, the firm's galvanised products were held in high regard with the *Birmingham Daily Post* maintaining that, *'the galvanisers report a steady business, and the galvanised sheets turned out at the Albert Works, Moxley, are increasing in favour in this market. Some very good orders have been sent down to this works for their galvanised sheets this week ...* '[355] In April 1878 the same paper declared that, *'there is a good stroke of work being done in galvanised iron, and fair orders were given out at quarter-day to Mr John Lysaght of Bristol; the Gospel Oak Company; David Rose of Moxley; Walkers of Wolverhampton; and other high-class makers well-known.* '[356]

David Rose continued to advertise for men and materials in other parts of the business during the mid and late 1870s with requests for a stock-taker, refinery workers, a boat builder and an overseer as well as for heaters for a mill and wrought iron for bars.[357] While he may have been recruiting, David was looking to hand over more control to his sons. In January 1878, at the age of 67, he gave over all the stock, machinery, wagons, locomotives and boats at the Victoria and Albert Works to his sons William and Henry. At the same time they were indemnified against five promissory notes to Lloyds Bank due for repayment from June 1878 to June 1882.[358]

The 1881 bankruptcy

In February 1881 it was noted that trade in the iron industry had picked up slightly and that some blast furnaces had been put back into service, including one of David Rose's.[359]

352. *The Birmingham Daily Post*, 13th April 1876
353. *The Morning Post*, 6th December 1878
354. *The Birmingham Daily Post*, 1st & 22nd July 1874
355. *The Birmingham Daily Post*, 13th April 1874
356. *The Birmingham Daily Post* 26th December 1876 & 22nd April 1878
357. *The Birmingham Daily Post* 22nd September 1874, 31st January 1876, 13th June, 16th July & 8th November 1878 & 18th April 1879
358. Walsall Archives and Local Studies, 48/39
359. *The Lichfield Mercury*, 25th February 1881

But there was no cause for optimism as the following month saw David file for bankruptcy as a result of a £20,000 loss in the previous year. His liabilities were estimated at £40,000.

A private meeting of some of the leading creditors, called by David Rose, was held on March 21st when the firm offered to pay 12s 6d in the pound. However, from a balance sheet presented, the belief was that he was capable of paying in full. Discussion at a further meeting with the same creditors centred on the amount of money and property that David Rose had given to his sons over the previous years. This was estimated at anything between £40,000 and £80,000.

When the public meeting of creditors was held in Birmingham on April 11th, another balance sheet was circulated with Rose's solicitor, William Duignan, claiming that the first one was misleading. The 1881 census shows that David Rose was staying at Duignan's house - perhaps the two men were discussing the best way of presenting their case.

Rose's solicitors claimed that the value of the works was only £10,000 and that in total his assets amounted to £20,000. The chairman of the meeting, Alfred Hickman, himself a leading ironmaster, had a different valuation of the works which was closer to £20,000. However, Hickman stressed that it would not benefit the public if the firm went into liquidation and after further discussion it was agreed that David Rose would pay 13s 9d in the pound in quarterly instalments. Bearing in mind that his sons had benefitted considerably from property settled on them in the past, they were to ensure that the money would be paid.

Following the 1881 bankruptcy David was joined in business by his sons, Henry, William, and Arthur although it appears that they came in without any formal deed of partnership. The business struggled on and adverts continued to appear in the Birmingham Daily Post over the next two years for puddlers, shinglers and a clerk, as well as for equipment such as a twenty foot wrought iron shaft. However the perilous nature of the firm's finances can be judged by Henry Fullwood Rose's decision to pull out from the business in March 1883. Henry was no longer to have a share of the estate, ceased to be subject to any liabilities but received regular payments from his brothers, Arthur and William.[360] Henry was also indemnified from several other mortgages that the firm had taken out in the previous three years. By this time Henry had moved to Bath and was leading a life of leisure.

By the middle of the 1880s David Rose & Sons were in rapid decline. Although the firm had taken on the operation of the Rough Hay Colliery following the death of George Addenbrooke,[361] and efforts were made to re-open the Broadwater Colliery due to falling water levels,[362] neither of the Albert Works blast furnaces was in production.[363] It also appears that by 1884, the Victoria Works, with its ten puddling furnaces and three rolling mills, was lying idle as it was classed as giving 'no return.'[364]

360. S.R.O. D1317/1/11/5/5
361. Mines and Mineral Statistics, 1884, List of Owners, Mines and Managers in South Staffordshire; *The Birmingham Daily Post*, 2nd September 1880
362. *The Birmingham Daily Post*, 10th April & 26th May 1884
363. *The Birmingham Daily Post*, October 9th 1884
364. Mines & Mineral Statistics, 1884, List of Mills and Forges, p.66

Efforts had been made to secure operating capital. William Napoleon Rose had already taken out mortgages with the Royal Exchange Assurance Company in 1881 to raise £1,050, and made another agreement with a Henry Goodman in February 1883 to secure £1,500. In January 1884 the Rose family shares in the Midland Railway Company and the Great Bridge Iron Company were offered for sale.[365] In May 1884 William borrowed £7,500 from his brother George who had decided not to be part of the family business. In August 1884 another £2,000 was secured from the Staffordshire Joint Stock Banking Company. This was followed by mortgaging a policy on his father's life in 1885 for a further £2,000. In March 1886 William mortgaged two policies on his own life to secure £1,500 from his sister, Elizabeth and brother, George. Similarly, Arthur Rose had mortgaged three policies on his own life to secure £2,250 from his brother George.[366]

The state of David Rose's business can also be gauged from the fact that he had avoided paying the rates. There was some dispute about the amount demanded and David Rose intended to lodge an appeal at the Quarter Sessions. In the event he decided to pay the sum demanded which totalled just £81.[367] By January 1886 the business was reduced to offering sand for sale.

The 1886 bankruptcy

In April 1886 David Rose & Sons announced that they could not meet their engagements. On April 16th the firm handed control of the Victoria and Albert Ironworks to the Bilston Bank owing to a debt of £7,500.[368] The sale of goods began in the same month with the livestock being the first to go: *'Seven Capital DRAUGHT HORSES, Two PIT PONIES, together with twenty-six sets of Cart Tackle and Chain and Pit Gears and Tackles, seven Nosebags, twelve Horsecloths, Stable Tools and Effects; Rick of Straw to go off.'*[369]

Then in May a further advert appeared: *'To be Sold or Let, on Lease or otherwise, together or in part, the ALBERT IRONWORKS, consisting of five Sheet Mills, Plate Mill, two Forges (containing 20 Puddling Furnaces), with Steam Hammer; Galvanising Works, capable of turning out 130 tons per week (with capacity of ready increase to 200); ample Fitting Shops, Stabling, Offices & c; two modern blast furnaces, with Engines and Plant. The mills and forges are in complete working order. The Works are situate on canal and London and North-Western siding, cover thirteen acres, and are in a ring fence.'*[370]

The state of the industry at the time might be judged by the fact that there were no immediate takers since a similar advert appeared in October. During the second half of 1886 several hearings were held to wind up the business. The total liabilities amounted to around £20,000. The decline in the value of the business had been startling. William Duignan, the Roses' solicitor, detailed that in 1877 the Albert, Victoria and Moxley Works were valued at £116,000. By 1885 this had fallen to £60,000. In one session David testified that: *'All the money he had was 50s, and this he handed to his solicitor. All his private things were included in the settlements upon members of his family.'*[371]

365. S.R.O. D1317/1/11/5/2
366. *The Birmingham Daily Post*, 1st June 1886
367. *The Birmingham Daily Post*, 5th November 1884
368. S.R.O. D1317/1/11/1/19/9
369. *The Birmingham Daily Post*, 28th April 1886
370. *The Birmingham Daily Post*, 24th May 1886
371. *The Birmingham Daily Post*, 9th September 1886

In the meantime the Rose brothers seemed determined to try and claw back money in any way possible. They accused John Skidmore and John Cartwright of illegally taking coal from a colliery at Moorcroft and claimed more than £1,600 in damages. The case eventually went to the High Court which settled that the defendants had to pay for coal extracted since 1879.[372]

Between all the hearings, in September 1886 the stock and loose plant of the Victoria and Albert Ironworks were put up for sale: *'Comprising about 500 tons of Castings, 90 tons of Sheets, 30 tons of Puddled bars, 50 tons of tools, Fittings and Implements, 8 Railway Trucks, Locomotives, 40 Tramway wagons, 20 Sheet Trolleys, Drawing-out Wagons and Carts, contents of Smiths and carpenters Shops and Stores. 6,000lbs of Brass, 90 Coal and other Barrows, 20,000 Fire Bricks, 1,000 tons of Calcined Tap, 20 iron and wood Boats, many thousand feet of Pit Timber, old Engines Wheels and Engines, Wheels and Engine Parts, together with the Galvanising Plant, Vats, tanks, and a great variety of Stores, Tools, Implements and Effects.'*[373]

At one of the hearings an offer to pay five shillings in the pound was refused by the creditors. In September, the Registrar stated that it had been the fifth time the case had been heard and that he hoped that the next session would resolve everything. This was wishful thinking – the case was not finally settled for another 9 months. The Official Receiver argued that the firm knew they were trading as insolvents, that this was a serious offence and ordered an enquiry into previous settlements of money which David Rose made on his family as well as the title deeds of the debtors' properties. There was obviously a concern that creditors were being short-changed by the manipulation of assets by the Rose family. In the October hearing it was alleged that William Napoleon Rose had recently advanced money to Edward Smith, a Wednesbury tubemaker, which was strenuously denied.[374]

David Rose did not live to see the final outcome. In October he was seized with an illness which confined him to his bed and this illness eventually proved fatal. Whether this was brought on by the stress of the hearings is debatable. His death certificate reveals that he died from 'general paralysis.' This terminology was often used as a euphemism for syphilis.

The Official Receiver, a Mr Pritchard, eventually drew up a report and submitted it in April 1887. He stressed that the bankrupts had traded at a loss ever since they had entered into partnership with their father, except for a period of two and half years. They had had to mortgage their debts, and borrow money to pay wages. He regarded the settlements of money and property by David on his sons should be taken into account when a final offer was made to the creditors.[375] In the end, the Rose brothers appeared to get off quite lightly. The final ruling in May 1887 was that three shillings in the pound was to be paid and the bankrupts were discharged.[376]

The messy business was still not over. George Rose and his sister Elizabeth then successfully pursued Henry Fullwood Rose, their brother, for debts in the High Court in 1888.[377] The winding up of David Rose's estate took several years since his remaining effects were not sold off by his trustees until July 1893.

372. *The Birmingham Daily Post*, 14th August & 6th December 1886
373. *The Walsall Advertiser*, 4th September 1886
374. *The Birmingham Daily Post*, 5th & 7th October
375. *The Birmingham Daily Post*, 28th April 1887
376. *The Birmingham Daily Mail*, 11th May 1887
377. S.R.O. D1317/1/11/5/7

18. The legacy of the Roses

The end of an era: the economic repercussions

The collapse of David Rose & Sons was not an isolated case in the iron industry. The years 1875 to 1886 saw the demise of nearly all the iron works in the immediate area. The Monway Ironworks of John Marshall was shut down in 1883 and the Darlaston Iron and Steel Company also collapsed with severe repercussions on both Darlaston and Wednesbury.

This period was known as the Great Depression and it marked the end of the great age of Staffordshire Iron. The number of blast furnaces in the Black Country continued to decline and although production of pig iron was maintained through larger units, most of these were now situated in the Dudley area.

We have seen that even as late as 1883 well over one hundred men were still employed in the Moxley works. All these would have been out of work. The effect on the local economy of the closure of David Rose's works was immediate. In March 1887 a report appeared on the bankruptcy of a licensed victualler, Joseph Pearce, who gave the reason for his demise as, *'Depression of trade, and the stoppage of a large ironworks at Moxley'*.[378] The Rose furnaces were taken down almost immediately. Efforts were made to restart the Albert Works in 1889 by Richard Caddick as the Moxley Sheet Iron Company but they were closed down again in 1892. The works were then taken on by Messrs Dickinson of Wolverhampton but by February1898 they were again idle.[379] The Victoria Works were taken over in 1886 by Simcox and Horton but they barely lasted a year. The Moxley Works were in operation until 1891 and were then dismantled.

Yet there were some positive developments. The Victoria Works were restarted by William Wesson in 1898 and an ironworks, later known as Ductile Wesson, remained on the spot until 2008.

The Ductile Wesson Works in 2006

378. *The Birmingham Daily Post*, 15th March 1887
379. FW Hackwood, *'Olden Wednesbury'*, 1898

The galvanizing arm of the Albert Works was taken over by Frosts in 1890 and again survived through the 20th century. The sand beds were still being mined by Arthur Rose in the late 1890s.

As for the acres of land taken up by the various Rose mines, for several years there were attempts to keep some open. In July 1888 there were several appeals, lodged before a Joint Court of Arbitrators and Commissioners under the South Staffordshire Mines Drainage Acts, against the 9d rate set in the Tipton district. George Rose, who had taken on this part of the business argued that: *'the Woods Bank Colliery ... was not now being worked, but he believed that if it was to be graduated to 3d he might find a tenant.*'[380] The Woods Bank and Albert Collieries were indeed graduated at 6d per ton. There is no evidence, however, that further mining ever took place.

David Rose's legacy for the landscape

While the collieries around Moxley were never worked again they still posed a threat and still claimed lives. The Woods Bank Colliery featured in another accident in February 1889 when: *'The South Staffordshire Coroner held an inquiry on Monday, at Darlaston, touching the death of James Plant, a miner. Plant and another man were employed in cleansing the pit shaft at Woods Bank Colliery. He had to work in water and when ascending the shaft he became faint, and fell out of the back to the bottom. He was found at the bottom in the dying state. Death was attributed to concussion of the brain. A verdict of 'Accidental death' was returned.*'[381]

In 1891 neighbours of Jacob Grove, a greengrocer and his family, living at Catherine's Cross, were puzzled when the shop appeared to be unattended. *'Still being unable to make anyone hear, they went upstairs and there, in two beds in one room, they found Grove, his wife, two of his children – daughters of ten or twelve years of age- and a grandchild, aged about four years, all in an unconscious state, and some of them, at least, frothing from the mouth. The discovery occasioned considerable excitement, and four medical men attended and administered restoratives.'*

The cause of the stupefaction is a mystery, but the prevalent opinion seems to be that foul air from disused pits in the neighbourhood must have found its way into the dwelling. Whatever the cause, however, it was potent enough to kill a cat and two birds which were in the lower room, and also to make the persons sick who were in attendance upon the occupants of the house yesterday.'[382]

The legacy for the landscape around the Moxley and Darlaston area can best be summed up by FW Hackwood who, himself, borrowed the words of an earlier writer: *'The eye wanders over a vast expanse of grimy country, unrelieved by the blushing of the unspringing flower, and scarcely by the gleaming of a single blade of grass. Vast mounds there are, indeed, but not of turf or verdure. They are swollen, dusty heaps of coal, and the offal of molten iron, and the whole prospect looks like a huge grave-yard where some grim old giants of a bygone era lie buried beneath the blackened ashes of their own victims. There is a weird funereal air about the place, which to a quiet looker-on is very striking and full of mystery. Away, a few hundred yards beyond the ebony hillocks, rises a hollow looking*

380. *The Birmingham Daily Post*, 4th July 1888
381. *The Manchester Times*, 23rd February 1889
382. *The York Herald*, 24th January 1891

building as black as themselves, with a tapering chimney, like some gaunt devil with his best hat on, standing sentinel over these sable graves.'[383]

Underground fires, a product of coal mining, still raged in the area for years afterwards. In 1908 Bell Street Chapel in Darlaston was closed due to structural damage caused by such a fire. Even as late as the 1950s such fires still appeared. In 2000 a house in Hughes Road, Moxley, disappeared down an old mine shaft and in 2005 over 120 houses on the Harrowby Road Estate had to be demolished due to mining subsidence.

David Rose's children

In 1880 Henry Fullwood Rose had married Emilie, daughter of the late Mr Henry Stone. After removing himself from the partnership of David Rose & Sons in the mid-1880s he moved to Bath where his wife Emilie had been born. They settled at 93 Sydney Place in a fine Georgian town house which is now Grade 1 listed. The family also had a holiday retreat at Burnham-on-Sea. The local paper described it as an *'important freehold marine property, known as The Poplar Estate, at Burnham, adjoining the Esplanade, commandingly placed on the Bristol Channel, looking out to the Atlantic, with extensive sea frontage.'*[384] Henry died in January 1918 leaving over £4,000 to his wife.

An underground fire in King's Hill, Wednesbury (Courtesy Sandwell Community History & Archive Service).

George Rose was equally successful. Having become a solicitor for the firm of Duignan and Elliot, he married Duignan's daughter, Florence in 1878 and went on to be the Town Clerk at Wednesbury. George died in July 1897 from cancer of the kidney. He left £4,345 1s 3d to his widow Florence.

Following the bankruptcy William Napoleon Rose attempted to carry on a business and raise funds, still attempting to rent out or sell the old factory buildings and trying to keep up appearances. In 1894 William was advertising for a pleasure boat to hold six to eight people which would have accommodated his wife and five children. However, the extent to which the family's fortunes had sunk is reflected by the fact that his daughter Edith had already been advertising for employment as a milliner.[385]

383. FW Hackwood, '*Olden Wednesbury*', 1898
384. *The Bath Chronicle and Weekly Gazette*, 15th June 1893
385. *The Birmingham Daily Post*, 10th October 1893

In June 1894 he applied for a reduction in the rates charged by the Staffordshire Mines Drainage Commission at the Moorcroft Colliery which was lying idle. William eventually set up in business with William Brookes as a scrap iron and breeze dealer, although the partnership was dissolved in 1901.[386] By this time William had moved out of his father's old residence at Cockheath to a more modest house on Church Street in Moxley. The old house was sold to William Wesson who had taken over the Victoria Works. William was still listed as a cinder merchant in the 1911 census.

Arthur Rose still described himself as a coal master in the 1891 census but ten years later he was a sand merchant and had moved to a small house in Russell Street in Dudley. The family then moved to Garston, Liverpool where he worked as an inspecting engineer. He died in 1927 leaving £235 8s 9d to his widow and son, Clarkson Rose, a celebrated Music Hall entertainer.

David Rose junior was never reconciled to his father after the affair with Annie York although he was employed as an office clerk. He died in 1887 from bronchitis and brain complications. Elizabeth Rose never married, helping her father with his paperwork and looking after him until his death. She died in 1890 aged 43, from heart disease.

And finally

My direct ancestor was Henry Rose who managed the Eagle Ironworks for his brothers David and Daniel. He died in 1882 leaving the princely sum of £90 15s and 10d to his widow Mary. Within two generations this branch of the Roses was living in poverty in Darlaston.

386. *The London Gazette*, 20th September 1901

Appendix 1: List of known employees in David Rose's works

Name	Date Ref.	Role	How Known	Page ref.
Allen Thomas	1875	Miner No 1 pit	Killed	10
Baker Abraham	1855	Albert Ironworks	Donation to Patriotic Fund 5s	67
Beaman William	1855	Albert Ironworks	Donation to Patriotic Fund 5s	67
Beech Israel	1869	Weigher	Robbery witness	88
Bell Jacob	1868-71	Cashier Moxley Works	Truck enquiry	70
Bond Henry	1855	Albert Ironworks	Donation to Patriotic Fund 5s	67
Blakemore Joseph	1873	Miner/Doggie, Albert Colliery	Suffocated	61
Bradley William	1874	Albert Colliery engineer	Near accident	63
Branaghan John	1858	Miner, Green Dragon	Trial witness	60
Brant Eli	1863	Puddler, Moxley	Neglect of Service Case	73
Brettle Thomas	1873	Manager, Albert Colliery	1874 trial	61
Brown Edwin	1855	Albert Ironworks	Donation to Patriotic Fund 5s	67
Brown James	1858	Labourer	Coiner taken to trial	89
Bunce Joseph	1874	Roller, Albert works	Advert	30
Burke ?	1871	Worker	Truck enquiry	69
Butler John	1857	Deputy, Bradley Mine	Killed	61
Carter William	1870	16 year old boiler worker Moxley Ironworks	Killed	50
Chalker Albert	1864	Manager brick works	Gave evidence	87
Chavasse Joseph Henry	1874	Account clerk to Fletcher & Rose	lease	97
Cole William	1858	Asst Ground Bailiff, Fletcher & Rose Bradley Mines	Court case with Great Western Railway	20
Collins Henry	1855	Albert Ironworks	Donation to Patriotic Fund 5s	67
Collins Thomas	1863	Puddler	Neglect service case	72
Cuniffe M	1858	Loader, Bradley Mine	Killed	58
Cooper Edward	1855	Albert Ironworks	Donation to Patriotic Fund 5s	67
Cope Henry	1869	Boatman	Stealing	87
Cope James	1858	Ground bailiff Green Dragon	Trial witness	59
Cranage John	1855	Albert Ironworks	Donation to Patriotic Fund 5s	67
Cottam James H	1871	Store Manager, Moxley	Truck enquiry	70
Danks Vernon	1858	Butty, Green Dragon	Inquest	59
Danks John	1869	Miner, Old Hill	Inquest witness	60
Danks Michael	1855	Albert Ironworks	Donation to Patriotic Fund 5s	67
Davis John	1884	Watchman, Broadwaters	Killed	64
Diggett James	1855	Albert Works	Donation to Patriotic Fund 5s	67

Name	Year	Occupation/Location	Note	Age
Dolman Henry	1858	Miner, Green Dragon	Inquest	59
Eaton John	1852	Forgeman	Assaulted D Rose	72
Eccleston George	1871	Brickmaker/contractor	Truck enquiry	69
Edwards Thomas	1855	Albert Ironworks	Donation to Patriotic Fund 5s	67
Ellis George	1871		Truck enquiry	69
Essock Samuel	1872		Court case	85
Evans William	1863	Puddler, Moxley	Neglect service case	73
Evans John	1865	Engineer, Broadwater Colliery	Accident report	63
	1867		Assault case	
Fellows Isaac	1868	Engine tender, Moxley	Killed	63
Fellows Joseph	1868	Miner, Waterloo Colliery	Killed	58
Foster George	1873	Miner/Butty, Albert Colliery	Killed	61
Foster William	1873	Miner/Butty, Albert Colliery	Accident witness	61
Green Joseph	1856	Pikeman, Bradley	Killed	57
Hall John	1855	Albert Ironworks	Donation to Patriotic Fund 5s	67
Harris Edwin	1871	Iron roller	Truck enquiry	69
Harrison Myles	1871?	Forge manager, census	Obituary, 1895	
Hartshorne James	1855	Albert Ironworks	Donation to Patriotic Fund 5s	67
Harvey John	1868	Ground Bailiff, Waterloo Colliery	Present at inquest	62
Hayward John	1855	Albert Ironworks	Donation to Patriotic Fund 5s	67
Hazeldine George	1855	Albert Ironworks	Donation to Patriotic Fund 5s	67
Hazeldine Joseph	1870	Head Engineer, Moxley Ironworks	Witness at inquest	50
Hazlehurst Jeremiah	1870	Blacksmith/striker, Moxley Ironworks	Present at accident	50
Heburn William	1865	Fireman, Broadwater Colliery	Accident witness	63
Hemmings John	1869	Watchman, Moxley	Witness to stealing	88
Hickman John Thomas	1869	Pikeman, Old Hill	Killed	60
Hillman Josh	1870	Albert Works Galvanizing	Advert	30
Hitchen J	1857	Loader, Bradley Mine	Killed	57
Highway William	1855	Albert Ironworks	Donation to Patriotic Fund 5s	67
Hodson Thomas	1855	Albert Ironworks	Donation to Patriotic Fund 5s	67
Hosling Edward	1858	Loader, Bradley Mine	Inquest Witness	58
Holland Simeon	1869	Engineer, Moxley	Neglect of duty	75
Hudson George	1858	Loader, Bradley Mine	Inquest witness	58
Hughes John	1869	Manager, Old Hill Colliery	D Rose Jnr bankruptcy trial	95
Humphries William	1864	Puddler, Moxley	Inquest into death of Samuel Martin	54

Name	Year	Occupation/Location	Event	No.
Hunt T	1860	Collier, Moxley	Killed	57
	1858	Miner, Bradley	also gave evidence in Great Western Railway court case	20
Hurlstone William	1863	Puddler, Moxley	Court case	73
Johnson Henry	1869	Manager, Old Hill Colliery	Petty sessions case	60
Kelly Michael	1858	Loader, Bradley Mine	Killed	58
Lamb Joseph	1858	Loader, Bradley	Killed	58
Law William	1855	Albert Ironworks	Donation to Patriotic Fund 5s	67
Lees James	1855	Miner, Bradley	Killed	57
Legge Noah		Albert Works		
Lloyd William	1871	Puddler	Killed his Wife	85
Lloyd James	1871	Asst Puddler	Son of William	85
Lowe Samuel	1855	Albert Ironworks	Donation to Patriotic Fund 5s	67
Lunn Joseph	1858	Doggy, Green Dragon	Inquest	59
Lynall James	1868	Miner, Waterloo Colliery	Injured	58
Maddocks Thomas	1874	Sinker, Albert Colliery	Trapped	62
Male Joseph	1869	Doggy, Old Hill	Charge for neglect of work	60
Martin Samuel	1864	Ball furnaceman, Albert works	Died at work	54
	1855		Donation to Patriotic Fund 5s	67
Mills John	1858	Bradley mines underground Superintendent for Fletcher & Rose	Court case with Gt Western Railway	20
Mills William	1855	Albert ironworks	Donation to Patriotic Fund 5s	67
Norton John	1874	Albert Colliery, sinker	Trapped	62
Pearson John	1855	Albert ironworks	Donation to Patriotic Fund 5s	67
Pointon Christopher	1864	Moxley, underhand	Inquest on Samuel Martin	54
Posten John	1869	Boatman	Stealing	87
Poulton	1869	Ironworker	Holland court case witness	75
Powell George	1857	Watchman, Bradley	Witness to murder	
Prestidge Edwin	1873	hooker -n	Death	50
Pritchard Joseph	1858	Waggoner	Coiner trial	89
Pugh Samuel	1855	Albert Ironworks	Donation to Patriotic Fund 5s	
Rotchell	1884		Daughter killed	
Shann Thomas	1855	Albert Ironworks	Donation to Patriotic Fund 5s	67
Shepherd J	1857	Pikeman, Moxley	Killed	57
Shorthouse Thomas	1855	Albert Ironworks	Donation to Patriotic Fund 10s	67
Smith Samuel	1855	Albert Ironworks	Donation to Patriotic Fund 5s	67

Solomon Jabez	1855	Albert Ironworks Donation to Patriotic		
			Fund 5s	67
Stokes Richard	1863	Puddler	Neglect of service	73
Stokes Samuel	1858	Iron Worker	Train accident	86
Street John	1855	Albert Ironworks Donation to Patriotic		
			Fund 5s	67
Summer John	1855	Albert Ironworks	Donation to Patriotic	
			Fund 5s	67
Summers George	1855	Albert Ironworks	Donation to Patriotic	
			Fund 5s	67
Swift Benjamin	1855	Albert Ironworks	Donation to Patriotic	
			Fund 5s	67
Talbot Ann	1864	Brickyard worker	Stealing cloth	86
Talbott George	1855	Albert Ironworks	Donation to Patriotic	
			Fund 5s	67
Talbott Jabez	1855	Albert Ironworks	Donation to Patriotic	
			Fund 5s	67
Taylor James	1855	Albert Ironworks	Donation to Patriotic	
			Fund £1	67
Tinsley Josh	1855	Albert Ironworks	Donation to Patriotic	
			Fund £1	67
Toon Samuel	1863	Puddler	Neglect service case	73
Tranter C	1864	Collier, Moxley	Killed	62
Upton Henry	1859	Puddler	Neglect service case	73
Wall Joseph	1883	Manager, Moxley	1883 riots	77
		Ironworks		
Wall William	1858	Dirt carrier, Bradley	Killed	57
Ward John	1855	Albert works	Donation to Patriotic	
			Fund 10s	67
Webb Thomas	1858	Doggy, Green Dragon	Inquest	59
Whitehouse ?	1858	Doggy, Bradley mines	Court Case with	
			Gt Western Railway	20
Whitmore Samuel	1874	Chief Engineer	Near accident	62
		Albert Colliery		
	1855	Albert Ironworks	Donation to Patriotic	
			Fund 5s	67
	1864		Inquest into death of	
			Samuel Martin	54
Wilkes Samuel	1870	Blacksmith, Moxley	Striker, witness	69
Wilkes Stephen	1871	Worker	Truck enquiry	69
Wilkinson Isaac	1867	Sinker, colliery	Killed	62
Wilkinson ?	1867	Colliery worker	Working with father	62
Willets Adam	1863	Manager, Moxley	Evidence in court	54
		Ironworks		
Wollisford John	1871	Shingler	Truck enquiry	69
Wollisford ?	1871		son of John, referred in	
			Truck enquiry	69
Wollisford	1871		ditto	69
Woodhall James	1855	Albert Ironworks	Donation to Patriotic	
			Fund 5s	67
Woodhall Thomas	1855	Albert Ironworks	Donation to Patriotic	
			Fund 5s	67

Woolley Ann	1871	Brickworks	Commission report	65
Woolley Mr	1861	Brickworks	Census	65
Woolley	1861	Brickworks	Census	65
Wright Samuel	1883	Ball furnaceman, Moxley	1883 riots	77
York Richard	1863	Puddler	Neglect of service	73

Please note that many of these individuals are referred to directly in the text. Some of the names, however, appear only in the appropriate report referred to in the footnotes concerned.

Appendix 2: Inventory of the Moxley Ironworks (1875)

• One double power condensing beam engine having a cylinder 34" in diameter and working a stroke of 5 feet. Hollow stalk halves, Beam of engine with parallel motion at cylinder end supported upon cast iron frame with strong cast iron foundations - Governor worked from main shaft and valves by eccentric two force pumps for boiler and tanks.

• One firing boiler 35 feet long and 7 feet diameter and one firing boiler 35 feet long and 5 feet 6" diameter with float, safety valve, stop boxes, fire grates and all gearing.

162 feet 7 inch steam pipes

162 feet 3inch feed pipes

121 feet 10 inch feed and waste pipes from canal to condenser

Wrought iron tanks

Old wrought iron boiler as reservoir supported on cast iron columns

• Driving machinery consisting of one 8 foot crank wheel with shaft and carriages, driving wheel 10ft diameter working with 3 foot spur wheel, 12 feet fly wheel with shaft and carriages and pinion working into 7ft 6 inch wheel on a shaft with carriage driving sheet mill, all on strong cast iron foundations.

• Sheet Mill: 20 inch with crabs spindle and coupling box connecting with chilled rolls with housing chocks and brasses (rest crossed out). Two spindles and four coupling boxes connecting with pairs of pinions with housing glands and brasses and *one* (two x) spindle and *two* (four x) boxes connecting *hand rolls* (pinions x) with pair of 10 inch groove rolls with housings, chocks and brasses.

Small pair of shears complete working off end pair of rolls, backplates, screws and boxes, cramps and guard, spanners and iron work all upon a strong bed plate. Slow speed for running rollers.

• Heating Furnace with castings.

Red and white brickwork, fire grate and stack.

• Large annealing furnace with castings, red and white brickwork, fire grate and stack.

One pair of shears working off end of train. Blade broken of one pan. Two pairs of shears worked underground from eccentric on shaft, drawing rolls connected to a crank on shaft giving motion by means of wood rods to shears, beds, standards, arm steeling and pin for shears.

Powerful shears with horizontal arm worked by large cam complete.

Forge

• One double power condensing beam engine having a cylinder 22 inch diameter and working a spoke of 3 foot 6 inches, slide valve worked by eccentric beam with parallel motion on reeler air pump condenser and head boxes, cast bottom frames.

• Two furnace boilers one 6 (9) feet and the other 8 (10) feet diameter with safety valves, floats, slop boxes & c.

117 feet 5 inch steam pipes

117 feet 3 inch feed pipes

212 feet 4 inch blow off pipes

• Driving machinery consisting of flywheel on main shaft (with carriage) 12 feet diameter pinion, 5 feet diameter working into 10 feet 6 inch spur wheel on cam shaft with carriages and brasses, cam with arms, helve with hammer, anvil, cup and block, full harness to helve and bottom plate, cast bed plates to machinery and strong timber foundations.

• Forge train 10 inches with 2 (3) pairs of rolls and housings with chocks and brasses, fore plates, screws and boxes, cramps and guards, spanners and ironwork, breaking spindle and coupling boxes and pair of pinions and housings with glands and brasses all complete in strong bed plate.

• One Ball Furnace with castings, brickwork, fire grate and stack.

• Three puddling furnaces with castings, brickwork and firegrate working with boiler.

• Three puddling furnaces as above working with second boiler.

• Three puddling furnaces with castings, brickwork and fire grates working with two stacks joined together.

• One puddling furnace with castings, brickwork, firegrate and stack.
• Brickwork to the furnaces and two firing boilers with flues and 3 stacks.

Drawing Out Forge

• One high pressure horizontal engine having a cylinder 12 inches in diameter and working a stroke 3 feet, side rods and lever with slide valve worked by eccentric on fly wheel.
A beam worked by crank having at its other end a small blowing tube with valves & c, blast main and pipes connected therewith.
• Driving machinery consisting of a 7 feet 6 inch drawing wheel and 5 foot pinion shaft, carriage and brasses, 11 feet diameter fly wheel and 5 foot wheel to blowing apparatus, cam shaft with carriages and brasses, arms to cam helve, hammer and anvil, harness cup and block complete with iron and timber foundations.
• One high pressure beam engine having a 14 inch cylinder, a 3 foot stroke beam on reeler and slide valve worked by hand gears with force pump for boilers all on strong cast iron frame.
• One cylindrical boiler 20 feet by 4 feet diameter.
• One cylindrical 16 feet by 4 feet 6 inches
Fire grates, safety valves, floats and all other gearing.
101 feet of 4 inch cast pipes and
25 feet of 3 inch cast pipes
• Driving machinery consisting one 8 feet diameter and one 11 feet diameter, fly wheel, two 4 foot 6 inch, one 5 foot 6 inch and one 5 feet spur wheel on shaft with carriages and brasses, two helves with hammers and anvils, cups and blocks and harness complete with arms and shafts with carriages and brasses all on strong iron and timber foundation.
• Two heating furnaces complete with brickwork, castings and stacks.
• Two double geared iron cranes and
One double wood iron with chains.
Centre shears and gearing complete.
Two charcoal fires with castings and brickwork working into one stack.
Brickwork to boilers, stack and machinery.

Roll Turning Shop

• One high pressure vertical engine with 7 inch cylinder and 15 inch stroke complete on frame.
• Cylindrical boiler 17 feet long and 3 feet diameter with fire grate and fittings and steam feed and waste pipes.
• Roll turning lathe with bed, poppet, stand and rest and gearing.
Grindstone worked by strap.
Brickwork to boiler and stack.
704 $5^1/_2$ square feet cast iron floor plates.
Cart weighing machine with plate, arm and lever
Gas and water pipes throughout the works.

Buildings and Extensions

• Office with slate roof, doors and windows, inside partitions, floors, stairs etc.
• Coach house with doors and slated roof at end.
• Entrance gates and wall.

Roofs

• Slated timber roof over puddling furnaces on 4 cast columns 36 and a quarter inch x 16 inch span.
• Iron and timber roof over puddling furnaces on 3 cast columns 10 feet x 16 feet span.
• Iron and timber roof over puddling furnaces on 4 columns 20 feet x 16 feet span.
• Iron and timber roof over puddling furnaces. One column 17 feet x 16 feet span.
• Iron and timber lean-to roof 10 feet x 16 feet span.

Over Forge

• New painted corrugated iron roof with ventilator on cast iron principals 70 feet x 35 feet with wood frame outside on 4 cast iron columns; inside supported by hangers from mill roof.

Over Puddling Furnaces

• New painted corrugated iron roof with 6 cast iron principals, wood frame supported on 8 cast iron standards.
• Two roofs slated and iron on timber. 6 columns 20 feet x 16 feet span ends.
• Main hipped roof timber 'Queen' principals, slated on 10 cast columns and brackets and brick wall at end 112 feet x 46 feet span.
• Slated lean-to roof on brick wall 62 feet x 22 feet span.
• Brick foundations under the machinery, furnaces etc.

Drawing Out Forge

• New corrugated sheet iron on timber roof with brick ends 70 feet x 46 feet wide.
• Slated timber roof with brick ends and side and 2 cast columns over charcoal fires 20 feet x 23 feet.
• Small house with tiled roof, doors and windows, pantry, oven, closet and fowl pen.
• Stable and store rooms with slated roof, doors and windows.
• Small house with tiled roof similar to the above but rather better.
• Large dwelling house with all necessary outhouses and wall around garden.
• Stable with tiled roof, 6 stalls, chaff cutting room above, brick steps and wall around yard.
• Cinder building with tiled roof and old brick building at end of same.

Roll Turning Shop

• Brick building with tiled roof over engine and laths (?)
• Blacksmith's shop with slated roof, 2 hearths and chimneys.

Gas apparatus

• Two retorts and grates.
• Gasometer 9 feet high with wrought case 9 feet 6 inch diameter.
• Condenser and 2 small purifiers.
• (Brickwork to Retort and) stack 20 feet x 3 feet 6 inches.
• Slated timber roof (brickwork to meter and old wall).

Clay store
(Bull dog kilns. One with 9 holes and one with 6)
Old buildings (with skeleton roof) outside mill
 (Hovel with sheet roof by mill)
60 feet cinder wall with old gates
 (Small hovel with sheet roof for boat builders)
Pig yard with walls and hovel, sliding iron doors
Store room for sheets 32 feet x 21 feet x 10 feet with doors and co
Stove and flue
Small hovel with sheet roof for boat loaders
Two boats length of wharfing
Shaking barrels and carriages
Pair of squeezers with blade, bed plate and part of driving gear

Bibliography

Primary Sources

Archival Collections

The Archdiocese of Birmingham Archives
Birmingham City Archives, Scott of Great Barr: MS3883
Papers of Addison, Jesson and Cooper, Solicitors of Walsall: David Rose
Dudley Archives
Staffordshire County Record Office, Papers of Addison, Jesson and Cooper: D1317
Walsall Local History Centre
The Waterways Archive, The Canal and River Trust, Ellesmere Port,
Wyken Colliery Correspondence, BW83.
Wolverhampton Archives

Parliamentary Papers

Children's Employment Commission, 1842
Children's Employment Commission, 5th Report, 1862
Children's Employment Commission, 1871
House of Lords Reports, 1864
The Mining and Mineral Statistics of Great Britain and Ireland, 1884
A Report on the Truck Commission, part 2 special reports, 1871
First Report of the Midland Mining Commission, 1843

Trade Directories

Harrod & Co's Directory, 1865
Jones' Mercantile Directory of the Iron Trade, 1865
Kelly's Post Office Directory, 1845
Melville's Directory, 1851
Pigot's Directory of Staffordshire, 1835
Robson's Birmingham & Sheffield Directory, 1839
Slater's Directory, 1851
Slater's Directory, 1862
White's Directory, 1851
Wolverhampton Street Directory, 1868

Newspapers & Periodicals

Aris's Birmingham Gazette
The Birmingham Daily Post
The Birmingham Daily Gazette
The Birmingham Journal
The Bristol Mercury
The British Miner
Chester Chronicle
The Darlaston Weekly Times
The Derby Mercury
The Dundee Courier
The Engineer
Journal of the Franklin Institute
The Glasgow Herald
The Grantham Journal
The Hereford Times
The Huddersfield Chronicle
The Hull Packet

The Illustrated Police News
The Leeds Times
The Lichfield Mercury
The Liverpool Daily Post
The Liverpool Mercury
The London Daily News
The London Gazette
The London Standard
The Manchester Courier
The Manchester Evening News
The Midlands Advertiser
The Midlands Counties Herald
The Mining Journal
The Morning Post
The Newcastle Chronicle
The Nottingham Evening Post
The North Wales Chronicle
Perry's Bankrupt Gazette
The Salisbury & Winchester Journal
The Sheffield Daily Telegraph
The Shields Gazette
The Staffordshire Advertiser
The Staffordshire Sentinel and Commercial & General Advertiser
The Tamworth Herald
The Wells Journal
The Wolverhampton Courier
The Walsall Free Press and General Advertiser
The Walsall Observer
The Wednesbury, West Bromwich and Darlaston Examiner
The Western Daily Press
The Worcestershire Chronicle
The Wrexham Advertiser
The York Herald

Church records
Registers of the Unitarian Old Meeting House, Coseley,
St. Leonards Parish Registers, Bilston
Christchurch Parish Registers, Coseley
Darkhouse Baptist Chapel, Coseley

Census records
Darlaston and Wednesbury 1841 -1911

Secondary Sources
Miguel Alexandre de Araujo Neto, 'Great Britain, the Paraguayan War and Free Immigration in Brazil, 1862-1875,' Irish Migration Studies in Latin America, Vol.4, No.3 July 2006
TS Ashton, 'Iron and Steel in the Industrial Revolution.'1924
Philip S Bagwell, 'Industrial Relations in 19th century Britain.'1974
George Barnsby, 'A History of Social Conditions in the Black Country in the Nineteenth Century.' 1980
George Barnsby, 'The Working Class Movement in the Black Country, 1750 to 1867.' 1977
Alan Birch, 'The Economic History of the British Iron and Steel Industry.' 1967
Marie B Rowlands, 'Masters and Men in the West Midland Metalware Trades before the Industrial Revolution.' 1975.

Elihu Burritt, 'Walks in the Black Country.' 1868

JC Carr and W Taplin, 'History of the British Steel Industry.' 1962

Nigel A Chapman, 'The South Staffordshire Coalfield.' 2005

SG Checkland, 'The Rise of Industrial Society in England.' 1964

Edward Chitham, 'The Black Country.' 1972

Rex Christiansen, 'A Regional History of the Railways of Great Britain: Volume 7 The West Midlands.' 1973

John Crompton (Editor), 'A Guide to the Industrial Archaeology of the West Midland Iron District.' 1991

Phyllis Deane, 'The First Industrial Revolution.' 1965

D Dilworth, 'The Tame Mills of Staffordshire.' 1976

DM Evans, 'The Commercial Crisis 1847-48.' 1849

DM Evans, 'The History of the Commercial Crisis 1857-58 and the Stock Exchange Panic of 1859.' 1859

JF Ede, 'The History of Wednesbury.'1962

Robert L Galloway, 'Annals of Coal Mining and the Coal Trade.' 1904

'Griffiths' Guide to the Iron Trade of Great Britain.' 1873

FW Hackwood, 'Olden Wednesbury.' 1898

FW Hackwood, 'Wednesbury Places, Faces and Industries.' 1897

Richard Hayman, 'Ironmaking, The History and Archaeology of the Iron Industry.' 2005

HM Hyndman, 'Commercial Crises of the Nineteenth Century.' 1892

DM Palliser, 'The Staffordshire Landscape.' 1975

WKV Gale, 'The Black Country Iron Industry.' 1966

WKV Gale, 'The Iron & Steel Industry, A Dictionary of Terms.' 1971

WKV Gale, 'Historic Industrial Scenes: Iron and Steel.' 1977

WO Henderson, 'Britain & Industrial Europe, 1750-1870.' 1972

Kinvig, Smith and Wise, 'Birmingham and its Regional Setting.' 1950

Oliver Marshall, 'English, Irish and Irish-American Pioneer Settlers in Nineteenth Century Brazil' 2005

Peter Mathias, 'The First Industrial Revolution.' 1969

Patrick McGeown, 'Heat the Furnace Seven Times More.' 1968

Harold Parsons, 'Portrait of the Black Country.' 1986

David Philips, 'Crime and Authority in Victorian England,' 1977

TJ Raybould, 'The Economic Emergence of the Black Country.' 1973

Bryan Reardon, 'Men of Steel.' 2012

Elizabeth Rees, 'Bilston in Old Photographs.' 1998

Ray Shill, 'South Staffordshire Ironmasters.' 2008

Harry Scrivenor, 'The History of the Iron Trade.' 1854

Malcolm Timmins, 'Street Names of Darlaston and Bentley.' 1993

Barrie Trinder, 'Britain's Industrial Revolution.' 2013

Chris Upton, 'A History of Wolverhampton.' 1998

JT Ward and RG Wilson, (Editors),'Land and Industry.' 1971

Kenneth Warren, 'The British Iron & Steel Sheet industry since 1840.'' 1970

Walter White, 'All Around the Wrekin.'1860

Ned Williams, 'More Black Country Folk at Werk.'

DC Woods, 'Customary Rights and Popular Legitimation.'

Websites
The Coalmining History Resource Centre

Index